THE BIBLICAL CASE FOR EQUALITY

An Appeal For Gender Justness in the Church

Belleville, Ontario, Canada

The Biblical Case for Equality
Copyright © 2002, Arden Thiessen

All Rights Reserved. No part of this publication may be reproduced, stored in a retrieval system or transmitted in any form or by any means – electronic, mechanical, photocopy, recording or any other – except for brief quotations in printed reviews, without the prior permission of the author.

All Scripture quotations are from the *New Revised Standard Version* of the Bible, copyright 1989, by the Division of Christian Education of the National Council of the Churches of Christ in the United States of America, and are used by permission. All rights reserved.

ISBN: 1-55306-343-0

**For more information or
to order additional copies, please contact:**
Arden Thiessen
P.O. Box 3045
Steinbach, MB R0A 2A0
Canada
E-mail: ardenths@hotmail.com

Essence Publishing is a Christian Book Publisher dedicated to furthering the work of Christ through the written word. *Guardian Books* is an imprint of *Essence Publishing*. For more information, contact:
44 Moira Street West, Belleville, Ontario, Canada K8P 1S3.
Phone: 1-800-238-6376. Fax: (613) 962-3055.
E-mail: info@essencegroup.com
Internet: www.essencegroup.com

Printed in Canada
by
Guardian BOOKS

Table of Contents

Introduction 5

   1. Discord in the Church 9
   2. The Varieties of Inequality 18
   3. The Church in the World. 29
   4. Listening to the Bible's Message 41
   5. How It All Began. 53
   6. The Culture of Male Supremicism 67
   7. The New Manhood of Jesus. 83
   8. Reconciliation Time. 100
   9. And Then the Spirit Came 113
  10. So Now There Should Be Equality 126
  11. Considering the Divergent Texts 134

Conclusion 152
For Further Reading 162

Introduction

WHAT YOU WILL READ here is the product of many years of reading, teaching, preaching, and pondering on the denominational policies and church practices that have restricted the role of women in the Church. I cannot even begin to give credit to all the people who have influenced my views and convictions, moreover, there have been many written sources that have had an impact on my thinking. Consequently, I make no claims to originality. It often seemed to me, as I was writing, that I was merely arranging and organizing ideas which had come to me from others. I have not used many quotations because my intention was not to write a book for scholars. Other writers have done that. However, regardless of the origins of my ideas, they have become personal convictions. I share them now with my fellow believers and invite them to consider again what the Bible has to say about the equality of men and women in the Church.

This book began as an essay and was not initially intended for publication. I started it as a personal monograph for my own benefit. I wanted to prove to myself that the biblical material related to the theme of male/female equality could be built into a coherent doctrine. Much of the debate on the issue, as I had observed it, consisted of presenting a few selected proof texts, which the opponents then countered with some texts of their own. I also wrote for the benefit of our family. Our children—three sons and two daughters, with their spouses—have often participated in around-the-table discussions about gender issues in our living room or at picnic sites. I wrote to clarify the issues we were discussing. They then read my early drafts, criticized, commended, and agreed I should develop my work further. Helen, my wife, who has worked by my side as a companion in my ministry, has also encouraged me to share this work with a wider circle of readers.

I am writing to my fellow believers out of my commitment to the authority of the Holy Scriptures. I have full confidence in their reliability and value. The inspired Scriptures must remain the ultimate court of appeal as we wrestle with the issue before us. I am, however, well aware that many readers who may share my view of the Scriptures hold to a position on the relationship between men and women that is very different from mine. I do not write to criticize or denounce. I am writing this as my confes-

Introduction

sion of faith; this is what the Scriptures say to me. I am inviting these readers to travel with me as I walk through the Scriptures and develop, in narrative form, the biblical theology of men and women and their relationship to each other in the church.

I do not write to enter into argument with other scholars who may have different viewpoints than I have. While I do occasionally mention alternative ideas, I do that only to clarify the arguments I am making and to help the reader understand the point of my discussion. Further, it is not my primary intention to criticize church leaders or denominational policies. Nor is it my purpose to find fault with versions of the Bible that have beclouded the issue at some points with translations that seem, to me at least, somewhat biased. My aim is to present to the reader the biblical narrative that depicts the theme of gender equality. Those readers who wish to skip the introductory sections can find this story beginning in chapter five.

I will not discuss the common questions about the authorship of the various biblical texts or the problems surrounding the integrity of the biblical documents. For some writers on male/female issues, these matters have seemed crucially important. I am well aware, and respectful, of higher critical studies. However, I take a canonical approach to the reading of the Holy Scriptures. With that, I mean that I accept the entire collection of Scriptures as God's word to us. I do that on the basis of the confidence of the early church; they were convinced that these writings, which we read and use today, were inspired by God. I trust my approach will be acceptable even to the reader who may not share my conviction about the nature of the

Scriptures. I see a unity and coherence in the biblical story which should be of interest to all those who value the Bible as a source for Christian thinking today

For the biblical quotations, I will be using the New Revised Standard Version of the Bible. My choice of translation is not significant to the outcome of my study. The doctrine I develop is not based primarily on the meaning of a few individual texts, on the nuances of interpretation, or on subtle connotations of the Hebrew or Greek words used by the writers. Grammatical and linguistic factors are, of course, important. The communication comes to us in sentences and words. Each grammatical and linguistic element adds, inductively, to the meaning of the total message. However, this total message which I develop here can be found in any of the traditional or contemporary versions used by Bible readers today.

This book was written in my spare time, over a period of several years. One advantage of such a slow and tedious development of the manuscript was that there were many opportunities to share earlier versions of it with friends. Their evaluations and criticisms have been very helpful. Two friends in particular—John Redekop of Abbotsford, British Columbia, and Jack Heppner of Steinbach, Manitoba—took the time for thoughtful and careful analysis of my writing. Their comments have made this a much better book than it would have been otherwise. I extend my thanks to them.

Chapter 1
....

Discord in the Church

THIS BOOK IS ABOUT men and women in the Church. We are all aware of the current controversy, addressed in many Christian publications, flaring up in most denominations, and wrecking the harmony in some Christian homes. It has been called a gender war. Wars are destructive. Wars bruise and ruin relationships. Wars usually violate common sense. However, wars may be terminated by a peace agreement. Opposing sides may learn to understand each other. This is why I write. I hope there will eventually be peace on this issue, not peace created by the triumphal victory of one side over the other, but the peace of mutual respect and appreciation.

I strongly believe that the Scriptures teach the full equality of women and men. God has no favorite gender. And I believe that Christian people, if they will be faithful to God, must declare this, teach this, and allow this equality to become visible in the Church.

This book is not a diatribe against denominations that do not allow women to be pastors. It is not an attempt to push women to the forefront and make leaders out of people who may have no interest in leading. I certainly do not want to make any woman feel guilty for not desiring a leadership role in her congregation. This book is an attempt to remove barriers that men, and sometimes women, have erected to keep women out of ministry positions. Most thoughtful readers will agree that any human regulations that limit or restrict the ways in which God can move and work in His Church should be challenged and examined.

The discord over the ministry of women in the Church has emerged in most Christian traditions. Recent Roman Catholic popes have encouraged the recognition of the abilities and intelligence of women for community and national causes, but they continue to maintain a woman cannot be a priest. The Southern Baptist Convention in the United States has recently made official statements about the subordination of women to male leadership. One of their better known members, former President Jimmy Carter, has publicly declared his disapproval of his church's position. I remember the Friday evening college dinner in Oxford at which the rector of an impoverished Anglican parish in Oxford explained he need not expect a promotion to a better church. There was no hope for his future, he said, because he believed in the ordination of women and his bishop didn't.

As far as I can recall, I have always believed in the essential equality of men and women. However, I did not consider or recognize the implications of this doctrine. On the issue of female leadership in the Church, I did as others before me have done and many still do. I hid behind the traditions of the Church and focused my attention on less controversial issues. As long as I have seriously read the Scriptures, I have been aware of the two restrictive passages—1 Corinthians 14:34,35 and 1 Timothy 2:11,12—which are discussed in chapter 11. These passages made it difficult for me to understand how the Church could hold to an integrated and practical view of equality. I am now ready, however, to share the details of the biblical unity I see on this issue.

I have also, in recent years, become deeply aware of the ugliness of the male supremicism I continue to see around me. I feel a need to respond to it. Further, I have been trying to overcome my strong inclination to withdraw from conflict and let others fight the battles. Since I have an aversion to saying things with which anybody might disagree, I have been silent when I should have spoken. I repented of that attitude and, consequently, undertook this writing.

Long before I gave serious thought to the relationship between men and women in the Church, I was suspicious of the doctrine of male supremicism. It was hard to believe that the Creator would have planned, and designed, women to be inferior to males. "Why did God need one sex to be in second place?" I wondered.

The Biblical Case for Equality

I was uneasy with the idea implied in religious language, expressed in Church structures, and insinuated by the way in which both men and women talk about themselves and each other: the idea that males and God have a unique similarity and a special relationship. Can it be that God has created a special club for Himself and all males, a club that excludes women?

Male supremicism did not seem to agree with the doctrine I was developing. I accepted an Anabaptist view of the Church—that the Church is to be a voluntary community of believers in which all members are to participate. Along with that, I adopted a charismatic perspective—that this community is filled, empowered, and guided by the Holy Spirit. Why does such a community need the tradition of male supremicism in order to be God's people and do God's work?

The lessons which I learned from the history of revival movements also troubled me. There have been occasions, from the second century to the present, when the Holy Spirit has moved in an unscheduled and unregulated way to revive the Church. Usually, women have been prominently active in these revivals. The consolidating of the effects of the revivals was usually done by men, and so the structures again became staffed by men. Even if such post-revival structuring would be seen in the most positive light—that it was done prayerfully under the guidance of the Spirit—we would still be left with the question: Why would the Holy Spirit use women in revival times and not later?

This book is not written as a feminist document. I do not think of myself as a feminist. I admit that feminism has many valid concerns. The goal of many feminists is

Discord in the Church

that women would be recognized as having the same value as men. With that goal, I am in full agreement. However, while labels are handy, they can also be tricky and misleading. The discerning reader will notice I do not agree with all that the label *feminist* may imply. I am well aware that, as I try to be true to the scriptural revelation, some of my arguments will sound feminist and may be used as planks in structuring a Christian feminism. My point is that I don't begin with a feminist agenda. My desire and purpose is to do an exposition of the biblical drama of sexual relationships without the distorting biases of male supremicism. We need to create an atmosphere of equality, respect, and mutuality which will allow the biblical ideals of peace and justice to be realized even between men and women in the Church.

I have been taking a long look at my innate sense of male superiority and my inherited association with the culture of male dominance. I don't like what I have seen in my life, and I don't appreciate the attitudes I have occasionally noticed in my male colleagues. I remember, with some revulsion, instances of humorous sarcasm or spiteful cynicism I have overheard at church events as men spoke to each other about the "women's issue." Generally, the issue was seen as a temporary pain in the neck, as a bothersome novelty which would eventually pass away as all fads inevitably do. It was regarded with an attitude of smug superiority, as something we would have to endure until conditions would return to normalcy. I remember such paternalistic attitudes with embarrassment. I have concluded that God did not create men to be superior to women and that it is, therefore, a sin if I treat women as subordinates. I believe that this new self-awareness is the working of the Holy Spirit in my life. And so I invite my fellow Christians to join me in this pilgrimage, this adventure of learning what it means for men and women to regard each other as full equals.

Every Christian is a theologian. With this I mean that all Christians think about the details and the meaning of their faith. Many may not be well informed. They may not reflect on their theology with a great deal of consistency. However, our loyalty to Christ should motivate us to work constantly at grasping more fully the details of the new life we are living in Him. You, the reader, have the liberty to think on your own and you may disagree with the convictions I share here. If they are not biblical they should be rejected.

I ask you, first of all, to consider the possibility that the doctrine of male supremicism may not be a biblical idea at all. In fact, I am suggesting that the idea of male supremacy is a secular social construction which has been with us, in our church circles, for so long it now seems perfectly normal and right. Our minds are in captivity to the cultural traditions of the past. We can all recall other preconceived notions we used to have but which we have now abandoned as biblically indefensible. Such changes in our Christian thinking are normal. Christian thinking requires the willingness to change. We should not reject concepts simply because they have a long history in the Church. However, neither should we assume that whatever is traditional must be right.

I do not need to argue for the intelligence and rational competence of women. The previous generation of writers on equality did that. In today's society, in which women

Discord in the Church

serve in all professions, in which women work side-by-side with men in business and government positions, and in which women often provide as much household income as do their husbands, the idea of female inferiority can hardly be entertained seriously by anyone. Some church people argue that, while the concept of female inferiority is a degrading and despicable idea, women must defer to male supremacy in the Church because that is what the Bible requires.

One of the rallying cries of the Christian feminist movement has often been: "The emancipation of women will require a new understanding of God." To that call, I respond, "Let's first take a another look at the Bible, at it's interpretation, and at the God whom we will then encounter." We don't need a new God. We need a new view of Him, one that is not tainted by male supremacist biases. To the woman who respects herself and has learned to think independently, the God who is preached in many churches may seem like just another male bully. We need to liberate God from the caricature imposed upon Him by His male defenders.

Some readers may have a prejudice against me because of my declared intention to be biblical. They may believe that the Scriptures are biased against women. Consequently, they cannot see how anything biblical can be fair. They may have developed their critical perspective because of sermons heard in church. I remember attending an evening lecture in Oxford on the subject of St. Paul's attitude to women. The professor worked her way through the letters of Paul and concluded that the apostle had already practiced and preached the doctrine of female equality. When she was done, a young woman in the audience cried out, in a voice cracking with emotion, "I don't believe it; I just don't believe Paul was that good!" I am writing for such women. I hope they will be willing to listen once more to the good news, the biblical good news of full equality.

I am also writing for those women who believe they are called to serve God and wonder why they are made to feel guilty about desiring to use their ministry gifts in the Church. Has God been playing a cruel joke on them? Does He give and then withhold? Does He give a gift of service and then forbid the serving?

I am writing for those female missionaries who are perplexed by the apparently contradictory system which sends them out, with the Church's blessing, to do among foreign people what is forbidden them in their home church. Women are encouraged to teach and preach abroad but are not allowed to do so in their home congregations. However, churches quote the words of Jesus: *"You will be my witnesses in Jerusalem, in all Judea and Samaria, and to the ends of the earth"* (Acts 1:8). That was said to both male and female followers. The Church's practice seems to suggest that the "unto the uttermost part" is for the women, but that the "Jerusalem" part is the male domain. What is the logic behind such a dissection of Jesus' words? One can even wonder if the current Church practice may reflect ethnic prejudices and be an expression of racism. Women are seen as unacceptable for teaching in their home community but are encouraged to teach other peoples, farther away. My book is a call to integrity in the Church. Do we have the courage and the honesty to look at our faith and practice

Discord in the Church

and then admit the inconsistencies? We believe we are the body of Jesus Christ. We call Him Lord. We believe the Holy Spirit is with the Church to direct, to guide, and to empower believers for service. Can we free our minds of restrictive and unbiblical taboos and allow the Spirit to lead us into a more integrated expression of biblical faithfulness?

I am writing for those, whether for equality or against equality, who sense that there is a conflict within the Scriptures and who have looked for a readable and accessible study on how the differing scriptural writings can be brought together. This is one attempt at such an integration.

Actually, this issue is important for the whole Church. Together, women and men in the Church must commit themselves to search for God's will and then agree that it must be done. If half of the Church feels put down by the other half, the Church cannot flourish. The apostle Paul wrote to a church that was in danger of fragmenting and argued, *"If one member suffers, all suffer together with it"* (1 Cor. 12:26). He has argued that all members are necessary for the health of the Church. There are no unimportant people in the Christian community. There are differences, he agrees. But he explains that when these differences are recognized and appreciated, they will enhance the strength and unity of the Church. He adds to the warning I quoted above, *"If one member is honored, all rejoice together with it."* It is as we respect and honor one another that we will become strong and united in our diversities.

Chapter 2

The Varieties of Inequality

BEFORE I PROCEED WITH the discussion of equality, we need to take a brief look at the various ways in which inequality has been expressed and practiced in this era of the New Testament. While I don't want this essay to major on denunciation or critical judgments, it may be helpful to understand, to begin with, what I regard as inequality.

It seems innate to human nature for people to group themselves in opposition to other groups within the same society. Such grouping or classifying is usually done to gain some form of power or control over another group. This trait can be seen among children on the playgrounds,

The Varieties of Inequality

among youth that roam the streets, among the different ethnic groups in a neighborhood, and between men and women. Invariably, one group will be seen as subordinate and the opposing group as dominant.

People who have studied dominant/subordinate relationships point out that the dominants always make the rules. They set themselves up as the authority for defining the acceptable roles of the subordinates. The dominant group also decides what relationship it will have with the subordinate group. After such dominant/subordinate attitudes have been entrenched for a while, it becomes difficult for the dominants to even imagine that the subordinates could be capable of the functions from which they have been excluded. Eventually, even the subordinates will question their own abilities. Further, what has been established and accepted begins to seem morally right. And so, both sides may feel that the status quo is how matters must be. Such situations are difficult to change because the dominants hold the power and have a vested interest in controlling the kind of power the subordinates have. Any suggestion of change seems like a threatening, dangerous, destabilizing idea to those in power.

This need or desire by the "in group" to protect their solidarity for the purpose of dominating or controlling, is essentially an evil trait. It is a social expression of human depravity. "May the best man win," is the rallying cry of this unholy power struggle. In this struggle, both sides always lose. Any grouping of people over against another group, whether along ethnic, lingual, status, or sexual lines, is ungodly. It is contrary to the community relationships for which people were created, because it always creates inequality.

The Biblical Case for Equality

What disturbs and alarms me about these social observations, is that the same phenomenon can be detected in the Church. Even in a church in which there are no racial or ethnic problems because the community is completely homogeneous, I hear reports of exclusion. Singles may say they don't seem to belong in a couples-oriented society. Widows have often told me they feel set apart. The financially disadvantaged may feel they carry some disgrace because they cannot flaunt their material successes. Those who are separated or divorced often feel like second-class members of the Church. Seniors may feel excluded by the new, youth-focused worship styles that are being introduced. In each case, one group feels itself disadvantaged simply because it is the wrong group. Some of the people in these stigmatized groups may have done wrong. They may be to blame for being different and not fitting in. Sometimes, they are ready to admit their faults. However, they will often conclude that their exclusion is based, not so much on what they have done, but on who they are. Such a rejection or demotion is particularly painful and frustrating because they cannot change the conditions upon which their reprobation is based. The traditional relationship between men and women in the Church reflects the same kind of inequality. By inequality, then, I mean any view of women which makes them automatically secondary to men merely because they are women.

I will refer, occasionally, to the attitude of arrogance and supremacy which men have often displayed in their relationships with women. Historians and sociologists have thoroughly analyzed and reported this aspect of the human story. In many cultures, men have assumed being

The Varieties of Inequality

male is being superior. They have taken rights and privileges which they did not grant to women. Often women have agreed to their secondary position. This sense of male supremacy led to domination. In some cultures, this has been relatively gentle and benign; in other cultures, it became cruel and violent. Such attitudes of gender-based pride are still with us. I recently watched a CBC documentary in which a husband from a non-Western cultural group defended his right to shoot his wife if she should ever commit adultery. Looking straight at the interviewer's camera, he declared, "Women are basically despicable creatures." Such blatant condescension is quite at home in the hearts of many men in our culture, too. Occasionally, it breaks out in the most horrific tragedies of domestic violence. This contempt for women sometimes leads to a generalized form of gender rage, as when Marc Lepine, a few years ago, took his rifle and stalked the corridors of a Montreal university, shooting as many women as possible.

Social historians have shown that women have usually been viewed as less than men (a good example of such a study is *The Subordinated Sex*, by Vern L. Bullough, Brenda Shelton, and Sarah Slavin, published by the University of Georgia Press in 1988). The history of women is a story of subordination and oppression. Men have often had an ambivalent attitude to women; they needed them as childbearers to propagate the race. However, they distrusted them and didn't quite know what to do with them in society. Women who asserted themselves and dared to think independently, unless they belonged to a religious order, were generally suppressed. Joan of Ark, who led her people like a man, could not be tolerated. The burning of witches, during the Middle Ages in Europe and later in New England, seems to have been motivated, not so much by the fear of aberrant dogmas, as by concern over the emerging prominence of women.

Unfortunately, the Church has usually echoed the values of society. I will argue, in chapters five to ten, that the Bible regards women and men as equal before God. This doctrine of equality can be witnessed in the history of the first-century Church, as recorded in the book of Acts. It is also evident in the teaching sent by the apostles to the churches. However, by late in the second century, the Church seems to have begun to succumb to the pressures of the surrounding society. This capitulation to secular values can be seen in other areas as well, such as in the eventual acceptance of military service for Christian men.

The Church's view of women soon became corrupted by Gnostic thought. Gnosticism is a philosophic interpretation of life, strongly influenced by Greek dualistic ideas. It saw a duality between flesh and spirit, flesh being evil and spirit being good. Sexuality, since it is of the flesh, was then viewed as sin. Since women are generally the object of men's sexual interest, they were then regarded as sinful and inferior. Celibacy became the highest virtue. Women, because of their "seductive powers," were satanized. Little hope was seen for their salvation. The gospel of Thomas is an example of the perfidious ideas promoted by Gnostic teachers. This document seems to have been widely circulated late in the second century. It is a collection of purported sayings by Jesus. It quotes Jesus as saying that a woman will have to make herself male in order to enter the kingdom of heaven. To the

The Varieties of Inequality

Gnostics, the circle seemed tidy and complete: sin equals sex, sex equals woman, woman equals sin. The early Church fathers couldn't separate themselves from this troublesome view of women. They looked at them as the source of sexual temptation and as a stumbling block in their search for continence and chastity.

Some of the early Christian leaders, men who are still admired for their contributions to the theology of the Church, made strange anti-feminine pronouncements. Tertullian (160-225), the great apologist for the Christian faith, declared that women are seductive, dangerous, and continuing in the tradition of Eve—misleading men. Augustine (354-430), the most influential theologian of the early centuries, saw women as seductresses and a threat to his new life of celibacy. He also opined that the woman, by herself, cannot be the image of God. She is to be married and then, together with her husband, she can think of herself as made in the image of God. What had happened to the high view of women expressed in the Gospels, in Acts, and in the early letters to the churches? It seems that, when it came to certain issues, the philosophies of the dominant Greek culture influenced, overcame, and transformed the theology of the Church. The Church was changed by the world. Christian leaders, trained originally in Hellenistic thought, brought these pagan ideas with them into the Church. Eventually, even Thomas Aquinas (1225-1274), revered as the greatest thinker of the Medieval era, agreed with Aristotle that the woman "is a misbegotten male."

It should be noted that women still received more respect in the Church than in the rest of society. However, from the year 200 on, there is no evidence that women had prophetic or priestly roles in orthodox churches. By then, segregated seating, as in the synagogues, had also been instated. The subordination and segregation of women had become an established and durable feature of the Lord's Church. This legacy of the past is still with us.

As I read or listen to the various expressions of male supremacy today, I often get the feeling that men are afraid. Maybe they are afraid of actually being inferior. Maybe they are trying to stack the cards against women in order to keep the upper hand. In other words, male supremicism may be a form of bravado to protect the turf that men have traditionally owned.

A modern-day tactic to promote the supremacy of men is to connect gender equality with homosexuality. Even though there is no logical relationship between the two issues, and even though the Bible does not connect them, some Christian polemicists have declared that equality is a gay issue. This seems to be a strategy designed to frighten concerned people away from the idea of equality. It's like guerilla warfare. It's designed to unsettle, disturb, and destabilize. Those believers who are already apprehensive about the erosion of traditional values, and who have been conditioned to mistrust anything new, may then decide to hide for safety in the traditional practice of inequality. This association of gender equality with the gay agenda is dishonest. It's an example of how the spirit of male supremicism, even in Christian circles, can become irrational and unreasonable. While such illogical accusations will not convince any thoughtful Christians, they may, however, turn seekers of truth away from the Christian faith.

The Varieties of Inequality

Another form of inequality, in contrast to the denigration described above, is the chivalry that places women on a pedestal as if they are more virtuous, more fragile, or more godly than men. Some women's groups have argued for such a female supremacy. And some men have agreed. At a ministers conference, I heard a senior pastor speak about "the feminine fruit of the Spirit of which we read in Galatians five." I suppose he meant that qualities such as love, joy, and peace (listed in verse 22) are more in harmony with the female nature than with the male's. His comment seems to imply that women are, by nature, more spiritual than men. Or, I wonder, was the statement meant as an excuse for the paucity of these spiritual qualities among men? Did he mean to imply that if these traits are feminine, we need not expect men to practice them?

One of the more disgusting forms of inequality is pornography. Most women find it offensive and degrading to be valued only for the sum of their body parts. Pornography drives a wedge between the woman's existence as a full human and her existence as a sexual being. It treats the woman, not as a person, but as an object which is best seen unclothed. Pornography says that what matters is the physical shape, not the other and more important human qualities. That is derogatory and demeaning; it deprives both, the woman who is desired for her physical qualities and the male who lusts after her, of their full humanness.

Some men will say that, when I speak of male supremacy I miss the point, because the real issue is that women are actually inferior to men. They will argue that they are not proud of their superiority; they are simply being realistic. We can't expect women to be our equals and neither does God, they explain. In a discussion group on gender issues, a man said, "I have a greater responsibility to God than does my wife." I admired his gallantry but questioned his perspective on female accountability. A man in my office argued that women should not be given positions of leadership in the Church because they are intellectually inferior to men. He supported this by explaining that most inventions in history have been made by men. A student in my class declared that women are too emotional to be church leaders. She said her church had been wrecked by emotional women. To which I responded, of course, that there are also churches which have been ruined by obstinate, unemotional men.

For most of us, the inequality we know has been inherited from the past, along with other cultural values and traditions. Equality or inequality was not an issue for most of our grandparents. They simply lived together in their homes and worshiped in their churches as all other people did. It was clear to them which was the woman's role and which were the man's prerogatives and responsibilities. As long as both accepted their positions, they could live together in a relatively pleasant state of companionship. Many people of that era probably did not think of their relationship as being unequal. Some readers will think of those times fondly; they will wish those conditions could be maintained in our time.

Customs, it must be understood, always keep changing. In some cultures, they change more rapidly and more painlessly than in others. Churches have generally been cautious about allowing change. This conservatism has often been good. Churches have been a stabilizing factor in

The Varieties of Inequality

times of rapid change and have kept cultures from disintegrating. However, churches or other religious groups have sometimes dug in their heels and ruled out change on particular issues. The official limitations on the role of women in the Church, which various church bodies have made in recent years, are of this kind. Inequality in the Church has been legislated into formal and official doctrine. It has been made the rule. The cultural customs of the past have been seen as sacred and have been constituted as law. Customs are flexible and fluid. They may exert great power over people but they may also bend and be adjusted to changing circumstances. Once they are enacted as laws, they soon become oppressive and discriminatory.

In most church communities today, women are seen as fully human and they are granted spiritual equality, in contrast to the derogatory views of the early Church leaders mentioned above. However, in many circles, they are not granted a practical equality. They are assigned a theoretical equality but forbidden to act as equals.

This dogmatized inequality reminds me more of Friedrich Nietzsche than of New Testament Christianity. Nietzsche, "the great antichrist" of nineteenth century German philosophy, argued that equality between men and women is impossible. Already in his day, he attacked feminism and declared that, with democracy and Christianity, it was leading civilization down into decadence and socialism. His ideal was the autocratic superman. Woman, he opined, has an instinct for the secondary role. He said women have no interest in truth and are not capable of understanding truth. He approved heartily of the "church decree" that women should be silent in church. He adds that they should also be silent about politics and about themselves (this summary of Nietzsche's view of woman has been gleaned from his book, *Beyond Good and Evil*).

It would probably be difficult to prove that Nietzsche's atheistic male supremicism has filtered down over the years and that modern believers have inherited their purported convictions from him. But the similarities are arresting and disturbing. I find it surprising and distressing that fellow believers sometimes sound more like followers of Nietzsche than disciples of Jesus. I had almost finished this essay when I discovered that Miroslav Volf, the Croatian theologian, had written already in 1996:

> Does not Nietzsche say bluntly and irreverently the same things about gender that many Christians say couched in a rhetoric of love and shielded by divine commands? The most radical atheist and the most pious fundamentalist seem to agree—against women! (*Exclusion and Embrace*, p. 190).

The apostle Paul warns:

> *See to it that no one takes you captive through philosophy and empty deceit, according to human tradition, according to the elemental spirits of the universe, and not according to Christ* (Col. 2:8).

I suggest that the concept of male supremacy, whether expressed gently or violently, whether protected by custom or by dogma, is another one of those deceptive philosophies. It is deeply imbedded in human tradition and can keep us captive. But Christ has come to release us from such bondage.

Chapter 3

The Church in the World

BEFORE WE CAN THINK intelligently and biblically about the role of women in the Church, we must agree with God about the nature of the Church. The Church is God's idea; it belongs to Him. It is God's agent, through which He is working out His redemptive purpose for the world. In order for the Church to accomplish this, it has to be under God's direction. We believe that the coming of the Holy Spirit at Pentecost was primarily for this purpose—to empower and inspire and give guidance for God's work in this world.

This essay is based on this charismatic view of the Church. By using the word *charismatic*, I do not mean that

I act like a charismatic person or that I like everything that goes on in charismatic churches. I mean that our commitment and passion must always be to let the Spirit of God control the Church. We should be critical of traditions that restrict the freedom of the Spirit and cautious about rules or policies that might contradict God's will for the Church. We have no right to impose human prejudices on the Church, and it is not up to us to determine what the Church should be like in the future. It is not our Church; it is the Lord's. The Church need not be organized or regulated according to our tastes; it is the body through which the Spirit works in this world. Therefore, we must let the Spirit of God, who dwells in the Church, be its leader.

It is, however, necessary to have some guidelines and regulations. The Church's mission is not just to be here, but to work out God's will in this world. This work requires organizing. However, there seems to be a tenacious human tendency, observable throughout history, to regulate, organize, control, and promote the Church according to human visions of what it should be like and should be doing. People always want the Church to suit them. They want a church in which they will feel comfortable. Since human nature is susceptible to various prejudices, selfish attitudes, ungodly values, and self-glories, these may be reflected in the structures and policies which humans impose upon the Church.

I have already mentioned that, as a whole, the Church has a reputation for conservatism. The Church tends to keep things as they have been. I consider this a useful role. In times of social ferment and rapid change, it is good to have a stabilizing institution that analyzes innovations

The Church in the World

from a traditional perspective and cautions against hasty, unthinking alterations to social structures.

On the other hand, not all that is traditional is right and good. Not everything that has become entrenched in society agrees with God's will and serves His purposes. Some examples from the past, on which most of my readers will agree, are slavery, child labor, the incarceration of mentally ill people, and capital punishment for minor offenses.

Culture is a human creation. It is the creative way in which people have worked out God's original mandate that humankind have dominion over the world and subdue it (Gen. 1:26-28). All people have freedom to construct their own culture, the pattern which their lives will take. Religious people tend to assume their current culture has been designed and given to them by God. However, the abuses we see in other cultures, and that other people see in ours, have not been ordered by God. They are the result of the misuse of freedom which all people have under God's mandate. It is the height of cultural arrogance to assume that everything in our culture is as God wants it to be. Sinful people cannot design a perfect culture. Since all are contaminated by sin, sin will be a factor in every culture. It is, therefore, incumbent upon us to look at our culture, comfortable and right as it may seem, and try to appraise it in view of the story of redemption. It takes an unusual level of maturity and spiritual objectivity to be able to do this. It will never be an easy, simple exercise. What one person regards as an essential feature of an orderly and proper society may to another seem demonic and destructive. May God give us the gift of discernment!

The Biblical Case for Equality

From our present vantage point, it seems that the Church of the past has sometimes, in all sincerity, been badly wrong. Some of its past attitudes seem more satanic than godly. Some of its past actions seem evil instead of holy. The Church has sometimes endorsed prejudices that now seem intolerable. It has sometimes practiced a violence and a brutality that now seem more hellish than heavenly. We see, in the history of the Church, many leaders who have professed allegiance to the authority of the Scriptures but who seem to have been prevented, by personal prejudices or the cultural values of their day, from understanding the Scriptures they loved. Good creeds do not necessarily mean good conduct. Reverence for the Bible has not always been translated into reverence for human life. A pietistic profession does not guarantee a Christlike spirituality. We conclude from the study of history, and from the experiences of our own pilgrimage, that people who try to be right may still be profoundly wrong.

If this is how it has been with people like us in the Church of the past, would it not be wise to look at our present attitudes and policies with a spirit of humility and caution? Is it not possible that, even today, we could still be misguided on some issues? Shouldn't we always read the Scriptures, share our convictions, and listen to each other with an openness to truth? Isn't it possible that, in spite of our best intentions, some important truth may be eluding us? Isn't it actually unlikely that we should now have reached the pinnacle of knowledge beyond which there is no further growth? God may not be finished with us yet.

With this openness for which I plead, there must also be caution. People with an open mind may accept ideas

The Church in the World

that are secular rather than spiritual. The world in which we live is always an influence upon us. The Church does not exist, by itself, in a holy vacuum. It is in the world, which is where God needs it. The Church, according to Jesus, is to be the salt and the light of the world. This presence in the world, however, means that the Church may also be influenced and infiltrated by the worldly atmosphere. So we must always take care; the societies of the world must not be allowed to determine the values, principles, and agenda of the Church.

Since the Church is always in danger of being seduced by the world, it is possible that some values which it holds dear may simply be secular values. Secular values are difficult to notice if they have been carried over from a previous era. They may have been adopted because of the cultural influences of that age. They seemed to fit well at that time. They became integrated into the religious culture of that era. But today, because of a long and venerable usage, they seem sacred and inviolable. All churches or religious movements with a longer history have such sacred cows. Examining these traditions is a painful task. What has been with us for a long time inevitably seems right and proper. Could this be why the principle of male supremacy seems like such an essential pillar of the Church?

Permit me to take my reflections on the relationship between Church and society one step further. Being like the world is not always wrong. All of society exists under the sovereignty of God. While worldly society often seems to be in rebellion against God's law, it may, however, develop values that are right and sensible and happen to agree with what the Bible teaches. In other words, a practice or a principle need not be wrong simply because it happens to be in style in the world. Some of the values which contemporary society has, may actually make it easier for the Church to be obedient to the Scriptures than in former times. In other words, changes in societal values may open the door for the Church to advance to a fuller obedience.

At this point, it may be useful to recall the New Testament concept of the world. Several writers, especially Paul and John, see the Church as existing within the context of the world. This world is inspired and ruled by the prince of evil. Consequently, the Church must separate from the world and be different for the sake of loyalty to the kingdom of God. Christian people must not love the world or the things in the world (1 John 2:15). They are not to be conformed to the world (Rom. 12:2). Sometimes, this principle of non-conformity results in clear and visible differences in the ways by which believers and non-believers manage their lives. For example, there still are peoples today among whom women are seen as inferior to men and among whom it is regarded as honorable for the man to lord it over the woman. Christians in such societies, if they have a careful regard for the teachings of Jesus and the apostles, may be so unworldly they seem eccentric. To illustrate such a situation, let's imagine a young Greek man in Corinth shortly after the middle of the first century. He's a typical Corinthian male with a loose, libertarian, playboy attitude toward his own sexual interests. He recently heard some Christians witnessing to their faith in Jesus and was so impressed, he also declared himself a new believer. Nobody, however, has given him any instruction about living the Christian life. Fortunately, he is given a copy of the letter that the missionary Paul wrote to the Corinthian Christians a few years ago. There he reads these words:

> *The body is not meant for fornication but for the Lord.... Should I therefore take the members of Christ and make them members of a prostitute? Never!* (1 Cor. 6:13-15).

Suddenly, he realizes what a radical, counter-cultural lifestyle his new faith will require. It will mean being different, really different, and his old friends will regard him as weirdly fanatical.

We all recognize that Western society has, in recent years, become increasingly open to the involvement of women in the different aspects of life and culture. In many circles, the equality of women and men is now treated as a given. Some Christian people see a dilemma in this. How can we embrace equality? Must we not be different? How can it be right for us to be like the world? Must we not resist whatever is promoted by society? I suggest the idea of equality is not wrong simply because it is advocated by people who also have many secular values. The world may adopt values that are actually quite compatible with the life Christians should live. Imagine another character from the late first century—the Roman governor of Galatia, in the middle of Asia Minor. He is a tough, rigorous, law-and-order man, a true Roman. His responsibility to keep the peace in his territory causes him an immense amount of anxiety. The Galatians are, by nature, a restless, unpredictable people. Further, the province is constantly being infiltrated by the ideologies of the mystery religions from the East. His practical Roman mind can't grasp these new, exotic ideas, but they seem dangerous. Beside that, some of his citizens have recently been meeting to worship a new lord, one whom they call Jesus. The language these people use sounds treasonous. He's not adept at comprehending new religions, but politics he knows. He worships the emperor and demands political loyalty of all Roman subjects. He's certainly not going to allow any subversive political movement in his jurisdiction. He summons one of the Jesus people for an interview; under interrogation, this Christ-follower produces a letter he has received from one of their leaders, a Jew in Palestine named Peter. Suspiciously, the Roman scans the document. He can hardly believe what he reads:

> *For the Lord's sake accept the authority of every human institution, whether of the emperor as supreme, or of governors, as sent by him to punish those who do wrong.... Honor everyone.... Honor the emperor* (1 Peter 2:13-17).

"Hey," he cries, "This reads like an edict from the Imperial Palace. You guys are as Roman as the Romans. I like this."

Regardless of what we see in the world around us, we should always take the cues for our conduct from the Holy Scriptures. Sometimes, that will mean a lifestyle that is drastically different from that of the world. Sometimes, however, the conduct that is patterned after the teachings of the Scriptures may resemble the practices of the world; it may even seem that the sovereign God is prodding and prompting us, through the values of the world, to reconsider the

The Church in the World

way we have been interpreting the Scriptures. Both experiences, that of resembling the world on the one hand, or being noticeably different on the other, may be the result of a faithful adherence to the Word of God.

Because we live in the world, we are always liable to adopt the thought patterns of the world. When we do that, we may not realize what we have done. Since we are then nicely compatible with the world, the wrongness of our thinking may not seem wrong to us. I will mention here three non-Christian paradigms that may keep us from thinking correctly about the right relationship between women and men in the Church. These paradigms, or thinking patterns, are common in the culture around us and have, in many cases, been unthinkingly accepted by Christian people. In order to think biblically, a paradigm shift is necessary.

The first paradigm that needs to be challenged is the idea that leadership requires power and authority. The common idea is that orderly society needs structures in which some people have power over others and have the right to control them. Jesus taught His disciples that this is not the way it is to be in the kingdom of God. When the disciples were angry because James and John wanted Jesus to promise them positions of authority, He explained:

> *You know that among the Gentiles those whom they recognize as their rulers lord it over them, and their great ones are tyrants over them. But it is not so among you; but whoever wishes to become great among you must be your servant, and whoever wishes to be first among you must be*

slave of all. For the Son of man came not to be served but to serve, and to give his life a ransom for many (Mark 10:42-45).

At the final Passover meal, as that event is described in Luke 22:24-27, Jesus overheard the disciples arguing about which of them was the greatest. Again Jesus corrected their thinking:

The kings of the Gentiles lord it over them; and those in authority over them are called benefactors. But not so with you; rather the greatest among you must become like the youngest, and the leader like the one who serves.

As John reports on that Passover evening, he described Jesus taking a basin of water and washing the feet of His followers. Then Jesus explained that they were to follow His example and wash one another's feet. If He has done it, they must also, because *"servants are not greater than their master"* (John 13:16). These passages reveal what I mean by a paradigm shift. The disciples had to start thinking in a new way about leadership if they were to serve Him. Leadership is serving. With this teaching, He turned their thinking upside down. Later in this book, I will point out that this paradigm shift is also necessary to comprehend the biblical teaching about the leadership of men and women. We need to learn to minister as Paul did. Writing to the Thessalonians, he recalled his service among them: *"We might have made demands as apostles of Christ. But we were gentle among you, like a nurse tenderly caring for her own children"* (1 Thess. 2:7).

The Church in the World

The second paradigm I mention, closely related to the one discussed above, is that people normally think they need to love themselves. Self-love is natural. In our fallen condition, this love for ourselves often turns into pride and prejudice. In this condition, then, it seems legitimate to strive for supremacy. And supremacy means that there must be others who are secondary and less important. This desire for pre-eminence seems endemic in our society. We need the corrective admonitions of Jesus. He sums up His ethical teaching in one simple, but profound, obligation, *"I give you a new commandment, that you love one another. Just as I have loved you, you also should love one another"* (John 13:34). This love is to be extended even to enemies (Matt. 6:44). In that matchless song of love, 1 Corinthians 13, the apostle explains that love is gentle, humble, and considerate of others. The apostle teaches, in Ephesians 5:25, that husbands are to love their wives. It seems he realizes this may be difficult for some husbands to comprehend, and so he stresses it again in the most convincing way possible: *"Husbands should love their wives as they do their own bodies"* (5:28). Once a person replaces the natural appreciation for pre-eminence with a commitment to love all people as the New Testament teaches, any talk of supremacy and subordination seems distinctly unholy.

I mention one more ungodly, but very human paradigm—the confidence in our ability to reason correctly and form ethics by logic. This attitude needs to be changed into an openness to the revelation of God. I do not mean that we must stop thinking. I mean that we must be humble in our thinking. We must recognize that our sinfulness may affect our reasoning powers. What God has given us must be integrated into our thinking. We must allow God's Word to judge and correct the thought patterns of our minds. The apostle wrote to a church which was being infiltrated with worldly philosophies, and reminded them that in Christ *"are hidden all the treasures of wisdom and knowledge"* (Col. 2:3). He adds, *"I am saying this so that no one may deceive you with plausible arguments."* We also need this commitment to the wisdom of Christ to protect us from the false ideas that swirl around us. This leads us to the next chapter, in which I discuss the ways in which God's Word comes from God to us.

Chapter 4

Listening to the Bible's Message

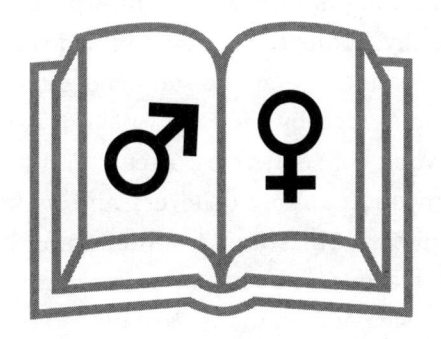

I AM WRITING THIS ESSAY under the assumption that some readers probably do not interpret all the teachings of the Bible as I do. I have already declared that I believe the Bible teaches the full equality of men and women. Some readers may hold to the secondary role of women in God's order of creation and they will, therefore, believe that women should be silent in the churches. How can we hold to such contrary views when we read the same Bible? How is it that we disagree when we are sincerely trying to be receptive to the truth of God?

In this section, I hope to show that conflicting views need not mean that one side or the other must necessarily have a lower level of commitment to Christ or a lesser degree of loyalty to the Scriptures. And I pray that the reader will agree that, even when we do not see eye-to-eye on the meaning of the Scriptures, we need not despise each other or try to demote each other as inferior believers.

I am committed to the venerable Protestant concept of "the priesthood of all believers." Among other things, this doctrine means that every believer has the freedom and privilege of reading, studying, and interpreting the Scriptures personally. While this is a valuable principle, rooted in the New Testament view that all believers are personally indwelt and guided by the Holy Spirit, it can bring with it some grievous consequences. It can lead to a fragmentation of conviction among believers and make it difficult for equally sincere Christians to understand each other.

Before I discuss reasons for our differences, let me declare the basic position many Christians hold. We regard the Holy Scriptures as inspired by God. We have accepted God's authority over us, and so His Word carries authority. Consequently, we expect the Spirit will use these authoritative Scriptures to teach and guide the Church.

Professing confidence in the authority of the Scriptures brings with it a massive responsibility. We cannot use only a few favorite verses. We need to comprehend the total message, the overall scheme of God's revelation. Some people, who speak of their commitment to the authoritative Word of God, seem to focus only on those comfortable passages that please them. Their outspoken defense of the authority of the Bible may be only a smokescreen to cover up a disregard for the rest of the Scriptures which may not agree quite so nicely with their chosen positions.

Listening to the Bible's Message

Respect for God's authority means that we have to lay aside our prejudices and be prepared to reconsider our preconceived tenets of faith before we can correctly understand the Bible. Since that is difficult—we cannot separate ourselves from what we are—we should at least be willing to evaluate the baggage we bring to the Scriptures with us. And we need to help each other do that.

First of all, I suggest there is no such thing as a totally objective reading of the Scriptures. We always come to the Bible with prior beliefs. However, we can improve our objectivity if we make an effort to analyze the sources and influences that have molded our convictions.

Further, it may be helpful to realize that we always like to be right. Consequently, we read into the Scriptures what we have been taught about them. We tend to look for assurance as we read; we prefer the Bible to confirm what we already believe. Change is painful. So, rather than anticipating that the Bible will convict us and correct us, we bring our biases to the Bible and hope they will be endorsed. However, we agree that we are fallen people. We have departed from God. Further, we believe that the powers of ignorance and confusion have infiltrated the whole world. We live our lives under stimuli that are designed to mislead and confuse us about God's will. We are susceptible to error. It should not surprise us if the Bible does not always agree with us. Rather, we should expect that sometimes the Bible will shock and shatter us. In fact, wouldn't it be strange if it never happened? The apostle confessed, *"Now I know in part"* (1 Cor. 13:12). This is also true of us. With the apostle Paul, we are looking ahead to the time when this partial state of affairs will be done away with. In the meantime, it would be wise to be open to further understanding and growth.

It may be useful to remind ourselves that there may be much we do not yet know. We may be completely unaware of how much we do not know. I suggest, therefore, that if we are not sometimes astounded by what the Scriptures tell us, we may not be listening with open ears.

The Bible needs to be interpreted as it is read. Its writings come from different times and situations than our own. The message to the original readers must be studied and examined, and then that message must be applied to our times and situations. Since we are not perfect people, this process will not produce perfect results. However, the process must continue. And it should not surprise us if the continued reading, and the continuing interaction with other readers, leads us to understandings we had not grasped earlier.

One of the reasons the Bible needs to be interpreted is that on no issue is the total biblical teaching given in one coherent passage. As an example, to understand God's will on marriage and adultery we should not read only the one simple command against adultery in Exodus 20:14. God's will on the matter is developed and expounded by many passages in the prophets, in Proverbs, and in the teachings of Jesus and the apostles. Interpretation means bringing together these various teachings from the different settings and seeking to determine how they should shape our Christian ethics today. Nowhere does the Bible have a simple and complete code of ethics that we can refer to as we do to entries in a dictionary. The origin and nature of the Bible demand it be interpreted.

Listening to the Bible's Message

Sometimes, people ask me, "Why don't you just read the Bible and obey it as it is?" My answer to that well-meaning rebuke is that nobody, absolutely nobody, reads the whole Bible and obeys everything "as it is." People who congratulate themselves on obeying the whole Bible can only be those who focus on a few verses that harmonize with their basic convictions, ignoring the rest. All readers of the Bible, even the most committed literalists, interpret as they read. Often they do so unthinkingly, especially when reading familiar figures of speech. They read, *"The Lord is my shepherd"* (Psa. 23:1), and interpret it as meaning that God cares for us. They may not realize that, for somebody else, "shepherd" may have entirely different connotations. Both in my classroom work and in my church teaching, I have noticed that, when I ask, "What does this verse say?" I often get an interpretation. For some reason, both college students and senior Bible readers tend to interpret when I am only asking them to read objectively and tell me what they read. It seems to be second nature to interpret a communication even before we have determined what it actually says.

It is true, however, that the Scriptures often have to be interpreted before the words make any sense. Jesus said, *"Let your light shine before others, so that they may see your good works"* (Matt. 5:16). That seems simple enough. But then we read, in the same sermon, *"Beware of practicing your piety before others in order to be seen by them"* (Matt. 6:1). Immediately we have to interpret; does Jesus want us to be seen or not seen?

Sometimes, people who disagree about the meaning of a certain biblical theme defend their position by claiming there is nothing to discuss; they simply read the Bible literally, they say. By this, they imply they are more virtuous and trustful in their faith than I am. But as I listen to them, I realize they too are interpreting but from a different set of underlying presuppositions. For example, I will eventually suggest that 1 Timothy 2:12—*"I permit no woman to teach or have authority over a man"*—does not prohibit a woman from doing pastoral work. The literalist may say she reads that verse as it is and it forbids preaching by women. But I would then remind her that she has read nothing about preaching or pastoring or church leadership in that verse. What she has seen in that verse is an interpretation, as is my reading. How do we decide who is right? And how do we interpret so that we get the message which the inspired apostle would want us to have?

In this respect as well, the Spirit is the guiding light of the Church. Our prayer should be that we be teachable and open to the guidance of the Spirit. The Spirit can teach us as individuals. However, individuals can easily confuse their own ideas with the Spirit's teaching. So we need each other. The Spirit came upon the total Church at Pentecost and is now at work in the Church. Under the guidance of the Spirit, each church group should function as a "hermeneutical community." It is in our Christian groups that we should study the Word, examine our presuppositions, and explore its implications for us in these days.

While we should pray, and expect, that the Spirit would guide us into correct understanding and true obedience of the Scriptures, we must recognize that the meanings we see will depend very much on the hermeneutics (principles of interpretation) that we use. Let me list

Listening to the Bible's Message

five such principles that seem especially relevant for interpreting what the Bible has to say about the propriety of men and women serving in various roles in the Church.

First, we must think ourselves into the situation in which the Scriptures were written. We must respect the cultural and intellectual framework out of which the Scriptures come to us. The following mistake is commonly made: statements, stories, commands, or symbols are extracted from the setting in which they were given and then invested with the meaning which they seem to have for the contemporary reader in her or his particular setting. A new meaning is then substituted for the original, intended meaning. This practice violates the literary character of the Bible. The reader's frame of reference becomes then the arbitrary absolute which determines the meaning of the text. This is what James Sire, in *Scripture Twisting*, calls "world-view confusion." A meaning is attributed to the text which it could not have had originally. The fundamental rule, which should guide all interpretation, is that texts mean what they meant. A passage cannot mean today what it did not mean to the author.

A fascinating example of world-view confusion is described in Acts 17. The apostle Paul appeared among the philosophers at the Areopagus in Athens and shared the gospel with them. As long as he spoke about God, even though he spoke from a Jewish theistic background, they seemed to listen with respect. However, when he mentioned the resurrection, they scoffed. The Greeks, with their dualistic world-view, held that matter was evil. To them, death was the successful release of the spirit from its vile house of imprisonment, the body. The resurrection, the restoration of the life of the body, was to them an incredible, offensive idea. The beauty of death, as they understood it, was that one was then released, once and for all, from bondage. A gospel which promised a resurrection seemed to them like a sick joke. From the perspective of their world-view, Paul's talk about resurrection was so enigmatic they couldn't even begin to grasp its significance. According to their world-view, such a prospect was the exact opposite of good news.

Second, we must strive to understand the writer's purpose. What issue or problem is the writer addressing? What was the meaning or significance of the issue in that day? What is the general principle that lies behind the specific advice given here? What did the writer expect the original readers to understand? This requires that we try to comprehend the historical and cultural setting in which the readers lived. For example, why does Paul, in 1 Corinthians 7, advise against all marrying, whether widowed, divorced, or never married? What were his underlying reasons? What called for such drastic counsel, counsel which seems highly unnatural to many people today?

Third, what is the meaning of the words which the writer used? What did they mean for him and for his readers? For example, when Jesus condemns tradition (Matt. 15) and Paul approves tradition (1 Cor. 11:2), we need to determine what the word meant in each case.

Fourth, we need to pay attention to figurative language. The Hebrew people loved vivid, colorful figures of speech; read Psalm 18 for their fantastic descriptive picture of God. Then imagine what it would do to our image of God if every term in that Psalm would be understood literally. Figurative language can be just as true as literal

Listening to the Bible's Message

language. However, when figurative terms are taken as literal, they can mislead us completely.

Fifth, we must always consider the context of the words we are reading. There is, first of all, the immediate context, the pericope or passage in which the statement is found. A single sentence, taken out of context, may give a false impression of the writer's intention. Jesus said, *"Do not think that I have come to bring peace to earth; I have not come to bring peace, but a sword"* (Matt. 10:34). Taken by itself, this verse can give us a very distorted view of what the coming of Jesus was all about. It seems to conflict sharply with the angelic announcement that Jesus came to bring peace on earth. We need the context to give correct meaning to this arresting statement. I recall a friend from many years ago. I'll call him Mike. Mike and his wife had a rather freethinking, hedonistic attitude to life. Then they were confronted with the gospel of Jesus and both surrendered their lives to the Lord. A few days later, Mike's brothers came by to invite him to another of their customary drinking parties. Mike explained that he could not join them because the Bible forbade all contact with alcohol. His brothers didn't believe that the Bible could be so restrictive and challenged him to prove it. Mike turned to Colossians 2:21 and read, *"Do not handle, do not taste, do not touch."* The brothers were astounded and impressed. Mike was right, they agreed. The irony of this story lies in the fact that the passage actually means the exact opposite of what Mike read into it. The point in the text which he used is that believers are free in Christ and that they should not submit to binding regulations again.

The context also includes the entire writing of which the text is a part. We must consider that particular writer's purpose, the original destination of the book, and the specific meanings of the words as the writer uses them. The Bible is a collection of writings. There was no editorial committee to critique and revise the language the different writers used. Each writer used the language as he had learned to use it. I remember a seminary class in which a student gave a presentation on the subject of sanctification. He roamed all over the New Testament, picking some verses from Hebrews and other verses from Paul's letters, to build his doctrine of sanctification. When he was done, the professor gently reminded him he had completely overlooked the fact that the word has a very different meaning in the letter to the Hebrews than in Paul's writings and that, therefore, his essay was logically inconsistent.

Ultimately, the context which we must consider is the doctrinal structure of the whole Bible. It is my conviction that, on many issues, this is actually the place to start. The reader will notice that I follow this approach in this book. First, we will try to comprehend the total message of redemption and its implications for the doctrine of equality. Then, we will look at some individual texts that relate to the issue.

The examples presented above demonstrate that without a thoughtful and consistent procedure for interpreting the Bible, it may seem to be filled with contradictory fragments of truth. Unfortunately, many readers turn to the Bible as if that is all it is—a book of fragments. To them, the Bible is just a collection of verses. There are two consequences of such an atomistic view of the Scriptures. On

Listening to the Bible's Message

the one hand, it may seem to be an incoherent hodgepodge of disconnected thoughts. The reader will then likely give up hope of finding any meaning in the Bible. On the other hand, there is the reader who desperately needs to find some guidance and spiritual help in the Bible. Such a person may then take a selective approach to the verses which are being read, developing a view of the Christian life with the verses that seem to fit, and ignoring the rest. And this illustrates, I believe, why equally sincere readers may come to very contrary convictions about how women and men should relate to each other in the Church.

Two other factors, besides the methods of interpretation we use, will have a bearing on how the Scriptures speak to us. There is the personal background the reader brings to the Bible—the experiences, training, knowledge, and mental facility. When we read the Bible, we bring with us all the convictions we have developed through our interaction with the experiences of the past. And we generally tend to use the Bible to reinforce what we already believe. This is why it is good to study the Bible in a group. In group study, we have the advantage of different perspectives. Further, a group made up of different generations may often be more helpful than a narrowly homogeneous group. This is also why it is beneficial to take into account the views of writers or commentators who explain the Scriptures from a non-Western perspective. They may remind us that the Scriptures need not mean what we have so easily assumed.

Another factor in the process of interpretation is the personality of the interpreter. One person may be gripped and absorbed by one particular truth; another, because of a different personality, finds another truth to be especially meaningful. I have noticed, for example, that some church people seem to be blessed by the theme of God's severity in the Bible. They see it everywhere, and they relish it. Others, reading the same Bible, are fascinated and amazed by God's grace and goodness.

For revealed truth to be understood, the reader has to have the necessary experience and imagination. For example, in listening to music, there has to be something in me to which the music appeals. If there is, the music will speak to me and, in the process, deepen my appreciation of it. It is also possible that some music may seem utterly meaningless the first time I hear it. But I may come back to it twenty years later and find that the music, which I couldn't appreciate earlier, is now right in touch with my soul. The music hasn't changed, I have. Our experience with the Scriptures may similarly depend on us becoming the kind of people who can understand its full message. Consequently, our different ways of understanding the Scriptures may not only be due to different levels of knowledge about ancient times and languages, or the different ways of interpreting that we have been using, but to the fact that we, the readers, are different people.

With these background ideas in our minds, I invite you now to proceed with me into the Holy Scriptures. I will not be comparing different interpretations, and I will not be arguing against those who feel comfortable with a different perspective than I take. I am simply asking you to consider a stream of thought which seems to do justice to all of Scripture and which is in harmony with God's desire for reconciled relationships between all people in His world.

Chapter 5

How It All Began

AS THE NAME SUGGESTS, Genesis is the book of beginnings. It depicts the beginning of human life in chapters one and two, and then, in chapter three, it reports on the beginning of human troubles. The story of God and His world begins, without any introductory words about God, in chapter one. In this chapter, the story is told in broad, sweeping strokes. The beautiful and profound creation account is developed in simple images, presented with poetic repetition. The chapter covers the whole scope of creation, from the original state of chaos to the creation of man and woman. The passage which concerns us for this study is Genesis 1:26-28.

> *Then God said, "Let us make humankind in our image, according to our likeness; and let them have dominion over the fish of the sea, and over the birds of the air, and over the cattle, and over all the wild animals of the earth, and over every creeping thing that creeps upon the earth." So God created humankind in his image, in the image of God he created them; male and female he created them. God blessed them, and God said to them, "Be fruitful and multiply, and fill the earth and subdue it; and have dominion over the fish of the sea and over the birds of the air and over every living thing that moves upon the earth."*

In God's creative plan from the beginning, there were two sexes—male and female. It is important to understand that both were created in God's image. There is no suggestion that one is more like God than the other. Together, male and female were to have dominion over God's creation; they were commanded to rule the earth. It was not given to the male with the female beside him as his assistant or subordinate. It was not given before the female was created. The man and the woman were both there when God said they were to have dominion over His creation.

The image idea, expressed here three times, seems to be of primary importance. God has an affinity with these humans unlike His relationship to the rest of creation. Because they are like Him, they can represent Him on earth. Their role was to have dominion, to be stewards, to function as caretakers for God. God has made them, both of them, for the same purpose—to be fruitful and look after God's world.

How It All Began

It is not necessary to "depatriarchalize" these texts, as some defenders of equality have proposed. All we need to do is allow proper hermeneutical procedures to bring out the message which was originally intended. This creation picture suggests nothing other than that humans, male and female, are equal in the Creator's sight. There is no reference here to any superiority or domination of the male. Nor is there any suggestion of female subordination. When such themes are seen here, they are brought from other texts. This passage, as it stands, suggests equal value, mutual responsibility, and equal satisfaction and pleasure to the Creator.

The story of the beginnings continues in Genesis 2. Actually, it seems to back up and repeat itself. The details, however, are very different. Trying to harmonize them with the previous chapter is a perplexing task. How should the two accounts be understood in relationship to each other? Scholars continue to examine and discuss the issue. Why are there two stories of creation? Why are they so different from each other, and can the two be harmonized in some way? It is not necessary to examine these questions in an essay of this nature. Without going into the critical details of textual analysis, I will simply treat the two versions as complementing each other, which, I assume, will be acceptable to most readers.

Chapter 1 looks at the overall picture of creation. It presents us with a philosophy of nature and of the natural world. It focuses on God, the Creator. It is because of His will and through His word that the world has come into being. Since all things have been made according to His will, it is a world of harmony and order. God is all-wise and all-good, and so His new world is a good and beautiful creation. The world belongs to God; He is Lord over it. Man and woman are distinct from the rest of creation and, under God's authority, they have dominion over everything else. The man and the woman are a team; together they will serve God and look after Paradise.

Chapter 2 of Genesis looks primarily at the creation of people. The first chapter says only that God created man and woman. Chapter 2 says that God made man from the dust of the ground. This reminds us that we belong to the earth. On the one hand, we are the image of God; on the other hand, we are made from dirt. We are earthly. Both the man and the woman are earthly. Since the woman is made from Adam's rib, she has, indirectly, the same origin he has.

But why was she made of Adam's rib? Certainly God could have made both ancestors of the dust of the ground. Since the many animals and birds are mentioned as being unfit to be the male's companions, this part of the creation account seems designed to demonstrate the essential oneness of man and woman. She is not an animal. She has a role that no animal can fill. And she is not to be treated as an animal. She is his kind of being.

Traditionalists who have argued for the primacy of the male have generally focused on the message of chapter 2 rather than on chapter 1. They have suggested three reasons why this chapter seems to suggest male superiority. First, they point out that, according to this chapter, Adam was created first. They assume that being first equals preeminence. However, the text, even in this chapter, has no suggestion of hierarchy. Rather, the central idea is that the man, by himself, is incomplete. In fact, the progression in the order of creation could be used to argue for female superiority. Creation began with inanimate life, moved on to living creatures, then to the male, and ultimately to the female. This is the way it stacks up, if we telescope the accounts of the two chapters into each other. To feminists who endorse this interpretation I also say, it is not the intention of this chapter to demonstrate that either sex has priority over the other. Rather, the purpose is to show why the human role in God's world required the two of them.

Secondly, those who support the traditional view point out that the woman was created to be the helper. They assume that being the helper indicates subordination. It is true that a helper can be a subservient person; slaves are often seen as helpers. However, the Hebrew word used here does not suggest inferiority, as the English word may. In fact, the Hebrew word is never used elsewhere of slave or servant help. On the other hand, a helper can be a superior, as when the Bible speaks of God as our helper. The word we are considering here is used fifteen times as a description of God. (See Exodus 18:4 and Psalm 33:20 for two examples). The word is normally used of divine help or of the military support that one people may give another, and there is no reason why it should have any different connotation here. Again, this point could be used to argue for the woman's superiority. Does God have to create a stronger person who will support the man in his weakness, one could wonder? However, the qualification in verse 18 refutes this tantalizing idea. The Bible I use calls her "a helper as his partner." Other translations speak of her as "a helper suitable for him." Whatever the exact translation, the term suggests that the man needed her, not because he was weak or incompetent, but because he had not been designed to be complete without her. The man had been created as a relational being. That's probably one aspect of being made in the image of God. Consequently, he needed someone to love, and it had to be someone of his own kind. What the man needed was not someone over him to supervise him, or someone beneath him to serve him. He needed someone beside him to complement him and live as his companion. The woman was not created to be the man's servant but to be God's servant alongside the man.

Thirdly, it has been argued that the man expressed his authority over the woman by naming her. This argument is based upon the scene in Genesis 2:19,20, in which the man names the animals. The naming of the creatures has been interpreted as an act of authority, as an exercise of the man's God-given mandate. However, as far as the text goes, the naming has to do with the differentiation between the man and the various creatures. None qualifies as his partner. When he sees the woman, however, he immediately recognizes the affinity she has with him. *"This at last is bone of my bones and flesh of my flesh,"* he cries (2:23). It should be noted that the naming of the woman, whether or not it suggests her inferiority, was only done in Genesis 3:20 after sin had wrecked the original relationship.

The man recognizes that he and this new person are one flesh. He declares, *"This one shall be called Woman, for out of Man this one was taken"* (Gen. 2:23). The narrator adds, *"Therefore a man leaves his father and his mother and clings to his wife, and they become one flesh"* (Gen. 2:24). I do not believe we can see here any suggestion of female inferiority or Adam's superiority. Rather, the passage describes an attraction that draws them together so the two become one again. It is impossible to speak of the dominant or secondary sex. They are one.

The narrator's explanatory comment about the man leaving his parents adds a fascinating touch to the drama described here. The patriarchism of most human cultures has required that women leave their parents and be joined to their husband's families. This traditional practice seems to suggest that women are of secondary importance. The formula announced by this writer, however, says man is the one who leaves in order to be joined to his wife.

It seems clear that this account, telling us that man was created first and then woman, was not designed to teach that one comes first in order of importance. The historical saga of male dominance and female submission begins only later. Here is described the most common of human urges—sexual attraction. It was a legitimate, God-created attraction. No sin was involved in their relationship at this point. They were made for each other. They came together and they were one.

With the creation of the woman, man had what was missing to that point. Man was not designed to be by himself. Man was made for the woman; woman was made for the man. Both sexes are fully and equally human, and human society consists of both. A society consisting of one sex only would be an incomplete humanity.

Chapter 3 in Genesis is the story of how it all went wrong. The woman and the man sinned. They ate of the fruit that God had forbidden. They yielded to the temptation because they wanted to become wise and be like God. The result of their disobedience was shame and panic; they recognized their nakedness and hid from God in fear and embarrassment. The original unity and harmony had been sabotaged. Instead of the spirit of mutual responsibility before God, there was guilt and fear. Instead of the previous unity in their partnership, there were criticisms and accusations.

God comes and calls for them. He tells them what they have done to themselves. Earlier He had said they would die; now He explains how. God says to the woman:

"I will greatly increase your pangs in childbearing; in pain you shall bring forth children, yet your desire shall be for your husband, and he shall rule over you."

Then God speaks to the man:

"Because you have listened to the voice of your wife, and have eaten of the tree about which I commanded you, 'You shall not eat of it,' cursed is the ground because of you; in toil you shall eat of it all the days of your life; thorns and thistles it shall bring forth for you; and you shall eat the plants of the field. By the sweat of your face you shall eat bread until you return to the ground, for out of it you were taken; you are dust, and to dust you shall return (Gen. 3:17-19).

It should be noticed here that God does not curse the people whom He has made and whom He still loves. He curses the serpent (v. 14) and He curses the ground (v. 17).

How It All Began

Adam and Eve had to live in a cursed environment. This is what their attempted autonomy would cost them.

As an aside, I suggest it is a sad and unfortunate development that theologians have commonly, contrary to the wording of the biblical text, called God's annunciation a "curse." With this label, His words have been seen as a penalty, predestining the people of God's world to live under His displeasure. God is then seen as being vindictive, punishing all of creation for the couple's initial act of autonomous insubordination. Rather, it seems to me that the passage should be seen as God's sorrowful recognition of the damaging, destructive results of human sin.

Let me summarize and list the details of God's pronouncement. For Eve, the consequences of sin are: 1) pain in childbirth; 2) in spite of that pain she will continue to have a desire for her husband; 3) her husband will rule over her (v. 16). To Adam, God says: 1) the ground has been cursed and he will have to toil to make his living; 2) the ground will produce thorns and thistles; 3) he will eat his bread with sweat on his face; 4) finally he will return to the ground from which he was taken (v. 17-19).

The interpretation of this passage is crucial to the argument of my entire book. The question is: Were God's announcements *normative*, that is, does He tell them how things must be, or were they *predictive*, that is, does He warn them about the way things will be? If the announcement is now God's revised will for His world, if He has reversed the conditions of Genesis 1 and 2, the arguments of the male supremacists have some merit. However, I will show later why I believe such an interpretation does not stand up to a careful reading of the text. In any case, the next question is this: Is this new situation for all of earthly time or is it a problem which is to be resolved under the cultural mandate which humankind has?

I will argue in this book that, not only is it our mandate to work at overcoming the consequences of the fall, God has acted decisively in Christ to make it possible. Most biblical interpreters have taken such a position on this passage. If the view is taken that women must, from now on, be subordinate, logically one should also insist that we must sweat when we work, that we must let thorns and thistles grow, and that women must suffer when they give birth. This, however, is not the view which Christian people have generally taken. I agree with the attitude of the Christian community toward the effects of the fall; it has usually been understood that God has given us the authority to manage our world in such a way that life may become less burdensome. My appeal now is that we be consistent and treat all the factors of God's predictions equally. I suggest that such a holistic view of this passage makes more sense and better agrees with the biblical message of redemption than the doctrine of male supremicism which has been extracted from these verses.

Let me present some examples of the intense ethical dilemmas which this passage has created for those who read the Bible literally and want to obey it conscientiously. I understand that, when anesthetics were discovered in the nineteenth century, serious questions were asked about whether it could be right to use this new medical discovery to alleviate the pain of women in childbirth. Some men argued that such measures were in conflict with God's will for women. Over the course of my ministry,

How It All Began

I have met various Christians who had anxieties about using modern inventions to make life easier and healthier. I recall concerns about immunizing children, about using birth control, about accepting treatment for cancer, and about using pain relievers. Often the argument was that what God has allowed we should not try to avoid. I have also observed that often these fatalistic restrictions were imposed upon women and children by men.

I grew up as a farm boy in Manitoba, and I still remember the year when the first herbicide came on the market. A neighbor bought a field sprayer and offered to spray our fields for us. In those years, wild mustard was a major problem in our grain. Here was a simple remedy. However, I remember that my father and some of his neighbors, all sincere Christian people, discussed the ethics of this new opportunity with deep concern. Could it be right, in view of God's word in Genesis 3, that weeds be eradicated this quickly? I am certainly not supporting the indiscriminate use of chemicals. I am sure that environmentalists have some valid concerns about the pollution of the earth by man-made substances. The mandate to have dominion over the earth cannot mean that God has given humankind the permission to ruin it. As a young boy, I knew nothing about the harmful potential of chemical pollutants. However, it seemed to me that there was no biblical reason why it would be worse to destroy weeds with 2,4-D than to kill them with a tractor and cultivator. I rejoiced with my father when he found peace over the matter and was able to use the new farming aid thankfully.

Those who still believe that the "curse" of Genesis 3 means women must remain subordinate to men, need to demonstrate that they also uphold all the other elements of that announcement. If they cannot, they need to explain on what basis they perpetuate one part and not the other.

I suggest that the passage we have been studying does not mean that it is now the male's duty to rule over the female, just as it is not his duty to allow thorns and thistles to grow. Both conditions are the consequences of human sin. Neither the male/female relationship nor the human/natural relationship will work as God intended it. Disharmony has been introduced into His world. The community which God created has been marred. The man has been corrupted into becoming a master and ruling over the woman. The woman has been corrupted into becoming his subordinate. God does not *prescribe* punishment; He *describes* consequences. He tells them what they have done to themselves. The people who rejected the harmony they had with God, now experience disharmony between themselves and with the natural environment. God's creation has been spoiled. Sin has been introduced and the Creator knows it will continue to have a painful, baneful influence over all creation. The goodness has been corrupted. Paradise is lost.

This passage in Genesis 3 is especially significant, because it gives us the basic explanation for all that is wrong with this world in which we now live. The entire environment, as well as all the relationships among the inhabitants of this environment, have been corrupted. As God explained, human efforts to subdue the earth will now be met with stubborn resistance. What was to have been a happy labor of love is now a painful, tiresome travail to stay alive as long as possible. In the end, however,

How It All Began

every person will be defeated by the destructive forces of nature and return to the cursed ground. It is a picture of despair, this routine of toil and struggle God foresees for His people.

However, there is no suggestion that we must fatalistically accept the spoilage of creation and suffer. The mandate of Genesis 1, that man and woman are to have dominion over God's creation, has not been rescinded nor has it been changed. It is the condition under which we serve God that has changed drastically. And so people, working under the authority given them by God, have developed labor-saving devices to avoid some of their sweating. Modern technology is the result. Chemicals have been developed, using materials God created, to subdue the thorns and thistles. Greater agricultural productivity is the consequence. Medical technology has greatly reduced the pain and danger of childbirth. Similarly, the enlightened world has taken large steps toward the emancipation of women from the fetters of subordination. In many respects, they are now allowed to live and function as equals with men. Unfortunately, while the Church has been quite eager to embrace the benefits of technological developments and accept the new amenities of life, large segments of the Church have felt constrained to resist the full liberation of women. It is strange and ironic that a church that can thankfully accept painkillers and herbicides and air conditioning still feels it is necessary to preserve and perpetuate the dominant/subordinate relationship between the sexes. Yes, God said of women, *"...and he shall rule over you."* But that is not a picture of how man and woman were created for the joy and satisfaction of the Creator. That is God's preview of how a sinful people will treat each other. In their attempt to be free of God's restraints, they have also ruined the mutuality for which God created them. They have decided to step out on their own, and God predicts it is not going to be easy or pretty.

Since these first chapters of Genesis are crucial to understanding the ideal and the actual relationship between men and women, I conclude this study with a simple summary: chapter 1—male and female were created in the image of God; chapter 2—male and female, distinctly different sexually, became one flesh in marriage; chapter 3—the harmony between the sexes has been spoiled by sin and it will become a painful, demeaning relationship. With this understanding to help us, we now look ahead. What happened next?

Chapter 6

The Culture of Male Supremicism

IN CHAPTER 2, I ALREADY referred to the gender inequalities that are evident in society as well as in the Church. I mentioned some of the striking examples of the disrespect which men have often had toward women. I designed that chapter to identify the disturbing features of our society which moved me to write about equality. This present chapter looks at the biblical record of male domination. We now ask the question: How did God's pronouncement work itself out for the people whom He had placed here to have dominion over His creation?

The history of the world provides ample evidence of God's foreknowledge. It has happened as He said. Thorns and thistles have infested the land (by the way, these terms are probably symbolic of all the other natural disorders with which this world is afflicted). Nature has not been kind; it has often acted like an evil enemy. People have felt threatened, abused, and attacked by the world God made. The goodness which was proclaimed by the Creator and which is inherent in nature itself, can still be seen as glimpses of beauty by those who look for it. However, often this beauty has been overshadowed by the violence of natural powers and the terrors they have created. People can, with modern technology, do wonderful things to protect themselves from the vagaries of nature. But they cannot change its essential character.

The apostle Paul describes the downfall of nature in Romans 8:19-23. The narrative of Genesis 3 is here given a theological explanation. The apostle sees nature as being in bondage. It has been subjected to futility. He pictures all of creation as longing for the time when it can be released from its curse and enjoy the freedom for which it was created. It is as if the entire world is groaning and laboring with birth pangs. Creation is suffering under the afflictions imposed upon it, just as are we.

Human life continues to consist of sweat and toil. These terms should be seen as symbolic also, speaking of the hardships, troubles, and futilities of life. The difficulties of life are reported throughout Scripture, freely and without apology. There is no attempt to glamorize life and pretend that pain, suffering, and death do not exist.

The pain of childbirth continues as well. Until recent times, every birth was seen as bringing with it mortal danger. Our genealogical records are replete with entries of mothers

The Culture of Male Supremicism

who died giving birth. Those who have access to modern medical care can now usually anticipate the bearing of children with hope and confidence. This does not change the fact that the consequences of sin are still with us.

The dominance of the male and the subordination of the female have also been an obvious feature of most cultures throughout history. Among those peoples who were strongly influenced by godly values, this relationship has been relatively benign. In other circles, however, women have been subjected to relentless suppression and unspeakable cruelties. They have been made to feel inferior and worthless under the debasing influence of male arrogance and domination.

In some sense, the ascendence of men over women has been due to the biological process of procreation. Women have, by their reproductive role, often been kept from activities open to men. Their slighter stature has also been a limiting factor in eras when success on the fields or at warfare depended largely on muscle and brawn. But the supremacy of men has gone much farther than that; men have insisted their role was to rule and women were to submit.

This prominence of the male over the female is depicted throughout the Scriptures as well. The cultures we meet in the Bible are no exception; they also endorsed and practiced the customary traits of male dominance and female subservience. God revealed Himself to such people. He chose such people and invited them to take part in His redemptive program. That people with sinful attitudes were invited to serve God, does not excuse such attitudes. Rather, it is a reminder that God accepts people with their sinful faults and works through them in spite of their moral handicaps. He still does.

The writings of the Old Testament preserve a view of women that is generally favorable to them. It is clear, though, that along with other Near Eastern cultures, Jewish society was dominated by males. Women had their place and were appreciated in the family. The virtuous woman of Proverbs 31 is highly commended, but even she is placed in a subordinate position, enhancing her husband's reputation from behind the scenes. While Hebrew women held a secondary place to men in their society, they were not, at least, considered to be God's unfortunate afterthought. Further, we can add to the credit of the Hebrews that they did not use Eve's role in the fall (Genesis 3) as justification for a negative view of women. In fact, Eve never functions as any kind of a female symbol in the Old Testament, as she did later in Gnosticism.

While the Hebrew people appreciated the role of the women in their families, women were excluded, by virtue of their sex, from social and religious activities. They did not normally have the same privileges men had in such matters as inheriting property, making vows, or initiating divorce. Occasionally, there are evidences that they were seen as the chattels of their husbands or fathers. In the Decalogue, the commandment against coveting lists the wife with the other property which may belong to the neighbor (Exod. 20:17). In Deuteronomy 22:20-21, the rule is laid down that, when a woman is given in marriage and then found not to be a virgin, she shall be stoned to death. Apparently, her sexual aberration was seen as a deadly crime because she did it while still her father's property. Nothing, however, is said

The Culture of Male Supremicism

about punishing the man who has been the other partner in her shame. Another example of this double standard is seen in the common prophetic practice of comparing Israel's moral lapses to harlotry, the deviant sexual activity of a woman (see Ezek. 16 and Hos. 1-3). The sexual deviations of men, which must have been just as common, are not seen with the same degree of condemnation and are not used as a metaphor for religious apostasy. When King David committed adultery with Bath-Sheba and then had her husband killed in an attempt to cover up the sin, the prophet confronted him about the sin that he had committed against the husband, Uriah. Nothing is said about his kingly abuse of the woman (2 Sam. 11-12).

The Hebrew rule about levirate marriages provides us with another example of the subsidiary place of women in their society. When a man died and left a childless widow, she was regarded as the property of her deceased husband's clan. She would then be given to a younger brother in order to raise up children to carry on the dead man's name.

This view, that women belonged in a secondary and supportive role, carried on within the traditions of Judaism into the New Testament era. Women continued to be seen in a decidedly inferior and subordinate position. The almost exclusive sphere of Jewish women was in the home. They were seen as the property of their husbands and treated as possessions which could be divorced almost as easily as other property could be sold.

To understand the male/female dynamics of that time, it is useful to consider their concept of group belonging. Some have called it "imbedded identity." Persons were not seen or known as individuals. Their identities came out of the groups to which they belonged. It was the father, the clan, the village, the ancestral origins, and the various historical connections which determined the identity of a person. This was particularly true of women. It was the woman's connection to a man—a father, a brother, a husband—that made her somebody. In keeping with this view of gender relationships, women had inferior status in Hebrew society. They were excluded from public life. Their most significant role was to produce male babies. Barrenness was considered divine punishment, seen as a damning and depressing affliction because it kept them from that accomplishment which could have given them some distinction in society. They were often treated as slaves by their husbands. They were commonly grouped with other second-class people; Jewish men would speak with scorn of "women, slaves, and children." (Historical material in this chapter is based, in part, on the article "Women" in Encyclopedia Judaica and on *Jerusalem in the Time of Jesus*, by Joachim Jeremias, published by SCM Press,1967).

The details I have presented in the paragraph above remind me of the speaker I heard at a men's conference. His purpose, it seemed to me, was to prove that a woman has no identity apart from a man. I suppose he thought this would encourage the men. He did a quick exposition of the word "man" in Genesis 1-3. The Hebrew word used in Genesis 1:26-27, sometimes translated simply as "man," actually means "humankind" since it speaks of both male and female in those sentences. Then, in Genesis 2:7-18, the same word refers specifically to the male in distinction to the female. Further, in 3:17, the word seems

The Culture of Male Supremicism

to be used as the name for the man, and the translators render it as "Adam" from there on (some translations already use the name "Adam" in chapter 2). After correctly explaining these details, he announced his deduction: "So you see, the woman receives her identity from the man." His logic completely eluded me. I had expected him to proclaim their equality, since both the male and the female are called "man" in chapter 1. As I reflected on his surprising conclusion, I thought of all the single women in our congregation and was glad they were not there to hear this deprecation of their womanhood. His opinion would have been perfectly at home among the Mediterranean cultures of Jesus' day. I was sitting in modern hockey arena, but I felt as if I was back in the Dark Ages.

In the biblical story, most of the rulers were men. So were the majority of the judges and prophets. It was a patriarchal arrangement. Men led the way and the women followed. There are, however, throughout the Bible, occasional variations of this cultural norm. I mention here three Old Testament exceptions to the usual practice of male leadership. First, there was Miriam, the sister of Moses (Num. 26:59). It is not exactly clear what her role was in the family trio that led Israel out of Egypt. But it seems she was up front with Moses and Aaron. She is listed, in Micah 6:4, as one of the leaders. When she was disciplined and demoted, it was not for stepping into a position that belonged to a male but for siding with her brother Aaron and questioning the unique and divine inspiration of her younger brother Moses (Num. 12).

All the judges from Moses to Samuel were men, except for Deborah. There is no explanation of her emergence and ascension to prominence; there is no word about who appointed her, how she earned her credentials, or how it happened that a male-oriented culture came to recognize her as God's chosen leader. But there she is, in Judges 4, sitting under her palm tree, dispensing justice, and calling and commissioning Barak to muster his army and fight the Kenites.

The third female leader I mention is Huldah (2 Kings 22). King Josiah had been informed about the rediscovery of the writing that contained God's law. He was greatly alarmed when the words were read to him and he realized how seriously his nation had transgressed. He needed spiritual counsel, and so he said:

> *"Inquire of the Lord for me, for the people, and for all Judah, concerning the words of this book that has been found; for great is the wrath of the Lord that is kindled against us, because our ancestors did not obey the words of this book, to do according to all that is written concerning us"* (v. 13).

And the five royal advisers, all of whom were men, knew exactly what that meant. They paid a visit to Huldah, the prophet of God. She is not introduced to us in any way; we are not told on what other occasions she had spoken or what she had said. We only read that, on this occasion, she declared as emphatically as any male prophet ever had, *"Thus says the Lord, the God of Israel: Tell the man who sent you to me, Thus says the Lord..."* (v. 15). The men took her message back to the king and he accepted it.

This case is especially arresting because it happened during the days when Jeremiah was one of the prophets

The Culture of Male Supremicism

in Jerusalem. The request for counsel was not brought to him but to the woman. Jeremiah must have been known to the king and his advisers; he was close to the civil leaders of Jerusalem, and he had already confronted them with his spiritual concerns. According to Old Testament historians, Jeremiah had been called to his prophetic role about five years before the incident described in 2 Kings 22. It is thought that chapters 1 to 6 in his prophetic book were probably preached before Josiah heard the solemn words from Huldah and began his reform movement. Jeremiah was the passionate preacher of righteousness and revival. From Huldah came the teaching and counsel which the king followed in his attempts to reform Israel.

None of these women had as prominent a role in the history of the people as did some of their male counterparts. None of them has a book to her name as do many of the other prophets. However, each of them gave leadership to the people. Each spoke words included in the permanent records of the inspired Scriptures. All three were accepted by their people and recognized as speaking for God. These ancient exceptions remind us that, while male-oriented cultures may suppress and restrict women in various ways, God is not bound by human restraints. He can transcend the customs and rules He has allowed people to develop for themselves. Whether we like it or not, we have to admit that, according to the biblical record, God's word has sometimes come to men through women.

The Old Testament has no word of rebuke or censure for these women who prophesied with authority, declared God's word, and taught men. They were, of course, exceptions. However, it is important for the argument of this chapter to note that these exceptions were made by God, not by men or women. God would not have made these exceptions if it had been His absolute will that women should be quiet and subordinate. God would not contradict Himself. And so, I suggest that these exceptions, which conflicted with the cultural norms of that day, were God's way of demonstrating that the conventions which people had developed did not really agree with His will for men and women.

The pattern of male priority is also evident in the many detailed Old Testament genealogies. Many mothers of famous sons are never even mentioned by name. Family lines are traced from generation to generation through the men. But then, occasionally, to our surprise, as if the inspiring Spirit wants to add some spice to a dull meal, there is included a woman in a list of ancestors (Matt. 1:5). One of the purposes of the book of Ruth seems to be to explain how it happened that King David had a Moabite great-grandmother. God is aware of the role of both sexes.

These divine exceptions continue in the New Testament. All twelve disciples were men. Many theologians feel there is an intentional parallelism in the basic structure of the two testaments. Just as the nation of Israel was founded by the twelve sons of Jacob, so the Church of the New Testament was founded by the twelve apostles. In both cases, the founding community consisted of twelve men. Further, as far as we know, all the New Testament scriptures were written by men. Some Christian people see these facts as having great significance for their doctrine of male supremacy. However, similar to the Old Testament, the details of which I noted above, the

The Culture of Male Supremicism

New Testament also reports on women who were anointed by God to speak His word to the world.

Luke opens his gospel by reporting the messages of three women, women filled with the Holy Spirit who spoke inspired truth. Elizabeth, the expectant mother of John, recognized that her visitor, Mary of Nazareth, was going to give birth to her Lord. She called her guest blessed, because Mary had believed the announcement which the angel brought to her (1:41-45).

Mary, the mother of Jesus, on hearing the affirming words of her older relative, Elizabeth, broke out in rapturous praise of God (1:46-55). The Magnificat, as her song has been called in church liturgy, reflects deep and profound insight into God's redemptive purpose for His people. Her song has a place alongside of the highest of the psalmodic and prophetic passages that envision God's saving actions in the future.

Anna of Jerusalem is introduced as a prophet. She spent her time in the temple, fasting, praying, and worshiping. When she saw the baby Jesus presented to the Lord, she broke out in praise of God and began to speak to all who would listen about the redemptive role Jesus would have (2:36-38). The apostle who recorded these words, and the Church that received them, seem to have had no problem with these unusual events. While men are prominent throughout the New Testament, Jesus was introduced to the world through the words of women.

That Jesus chose twelve male disciples, seems understandable in view of the wandering lifestyle their preaching ministry required. Further, men were more likely to have the education needed for their future leadership roles. The Jewish customs of that time, which I have discussed above, also necessitated that this intimate training group be made up of men. However, women were not excluded from fellowship with Jesus or from participation in His ministry. We don't know how consistently they were present, but there was a group of women who served and supported Jesus (Luke 8:1-3). Some of these women were with Jesus during the Passion Week; they were there with Him when He suffered and died. Later, they were part of the group of believers who met after the departure of Jesus, and they became part of the original Church in Jerusalem (Acts 1:14).

The historical stories of Acts give us the impression that the Church grew and spread through male power. However, now and then there is mention of women who were prominently active in the Church. It is reported that Philip had four daughters who had the gift of prophecy (Acts 21:8). It also mentioned that Priscilla and Aquila, a husband and wife team, were co-teachers in the church at Ephesus (Acts 18:26). In his letter to the Philippian church, the apostle Paul mentions two women who had toiled alongside him in his gospel ministry; it seems they had been part of a larger evangelistic team. However, he had heard that they were now at odds with each other and requests that someone help them with their differences (Phil. 4:2,3).

The last chapter of Paul's highly important letter to the Christian communities in Rome gives us further insight into the prominence of women in the churches (Rom. 16). This chapter presents us with fascinating insight into the networking growth of the Church in the first century. New

The Culture of Male Supremicism

believers moved, traveled, and made connections with relatives in other cities. Always they took the message of Jesus with them, forming communities of faith throughout the Roman Empire. And women were an important component of this growing Christian network.

To begin with, the letter was personally carried to Rome by a woman, Phoebe. She is introduced as a servant, or deacon, of the church at Cenchreae. It is this woman who was entrusted with the task of bringing this letter—the most important theological document in the New Testament—to Rome, the center of the Gentile world. Paul had never been to Rome. However, in his greetings to the Church, he recognizes at least seven female acquaintances who were important enough in the Church to be mentioned. There is Junia, who was prominent among the apostles (although this person's sexual identity is somewhat ambiguous because of textual variations in verse 7). There is Mary (v. 6), Tryphaena, Tryphosa, and Persis (v.12) who had all worked hard for the Lord. What was it these female workers had done? The word which Paul uses here, as he mentions their work, is a term that normally suggests difficult toil and labor; he uses it elsewhere to describe his own preaching and teaching work and the hardships that accompanied such ministries. I tend to agree with an earlier commentator I once read who declared that their work certainly would not have consisted merely of preparing chicken dinners for male preachers.

The New Testament references to the elders or bishops (pastors) in the early Church sound as if they were men. In fact, the instructions in the Pastoral Letters assume that these leaders will be men (1 Tim. 3:2,4).

With this, it should be mentioned that these letters also assume they would be married. These assumptions need not mean that they had to be males or that they had to be married. When the text says that the church leader must be the husband of one wife, the issue probably is not that this person must be a male, but that the male in this position, if married, must have a faithful and monogamous relationship. The apostle simply accepts the social realities of his day and works with them. The same writer also assumes that some believers will own slaves (1 Tim. 6:2). Nobody in our circles uses this assumption to argue that slavery should be practiced among Christians. We understand that this teaching about how masters are to treat their slaves does not give anybody the permanent right to have slaves. In this case also, the apostle accepts the cultural structures as they existed then and applies to them God's principles for maintaining gracious Christlike relationships.

Besides the references to male leadership, the Pastoral Letters also speak specifically of women who served in the churches. Their qualifications are listed in 1 Timothy 3:11. (The reading, "Their wives," which is found in some versions, is an inaccurate translation of the apostle's words; he wrote "Women likewise..."). Further stipulations on the kind of women who may serve in the Church are given in 1 Timothy 4.

It needs to be understood that these instructions to the Church do not necessarily picture the ideal; rather, they accept human customs as they were and spoke God's word to them. This is how God always works on earth. By God's grace, He can use for His purpose that

The Culture of Male Supremicism

which still is tarnished by sinful disfigurations. However, we should not console ourselves by saying that what God can accept must be as good as God wants it to be. His goal is to redeem men and women from the sinful accretions with which their relationship has been encrusted so that they can function together as His stewards in this world. That was His original intention for them and it continues to be His hope for the future.

The ascendence of men and their firm grip on supremacy is seen in the Scriptures from Genesis 3 to Revelation. Occasionally, however, the sovereign God surprises us. Sometimes He seems to snub His nose at traditional male dominance and do His work through women. He does not do this to upset the structures of society. That, apparently, is not His way. It seems He keeps on teasing us, prodding us, and challenging us to open our prejudiced eyes and notice He has made people both male and female, and that His work can be done by both.

What is the purpose of these exceptions we see throughout the Bible? Is it that, at these points, no men were available? Is it that, at some points, women stepped over their bounds? Did society occasionally fail and allow women to emerge inappropriately? The narratives do not read that way. Isn't it much more likely that God has a bigger vision than men and women have often had and that He was preparing people for the new society of the new kingdom which He would be building on earth? And isn't it very well possible that, throughout the history of male supremacy, God was already giving hints that a new era was on the horizon? Was God perhaps suggesting to the world that He has bigger and better things in mind for them than that which they had arranged for themselves? The biblical narrative responds to such questions by presenting us with the story of the new man, Jesus.

Chapter 7

The New Manhood of Jesus

JESUS APPEARED HERE TO make God known to us. He came from God to us; He stepped out of heaven to be flesh and blood on earth. His mission was to reveal God's will to us. What God had done in previous ages through the prophets, using them indirectly as His mouthpieces, He would now do directly through Jesus. When we want to know how people should relate to each other, we should, of course, read the prophets and the apostles, but we should also notice how Jesus did it. Jesus, with all that He was and did and said, is God's word to us. The letter to the Hebrews speaks of the various ways in which God spoke in the past to the prophets.

Then the writer adds,

> But in these last days he has spoken to us by a Son, whom he appointed heir of all things, through whom he also created the worlds. He is the reflection of God's glory and the exact imprint of God's very being (Heb. 1:1-3).

God has come to us in the person of Jesus.

As I mentioned, Jesus stepped into the historical and cultural milieu of this world as He found it. He was a Jew, a resident of Galilee, a son of the tribe of Judah. He lived among His fellow people as one of them. He was at home among the cultures of Palestine. However, by His actions and His teachings, He constantly critiqued and judged the structures He had chosen to join. The record of His life continues to confront all the societies of this world, including ours, with the invitation to rise to a higher level of moral sensitivity. His story challenges us to recognize how far from God's ideal we have drifted and calls us follow Him in a life that is properly human.

God has two messages for us in Christ. First, He wanted to show us what He Himself is like, i.e., He wanted to reveal His love and compassion to us. He wanted us to understand that He cares and that he is approachable. He wanted to show us in what way He is holy. Secondly, He wanted to show us what humankind should be like. It is important that we realize that Jesus was just as human as we are. Actually, we should say that Jesus was more human than we are. He was human the way God intends all of us to be human. These two aspects of divine revelation could coincide in Jesus Christ because, as the tradi-

The New Manhood of Jesus

tional Christian formula puts it, He is both fully divine and fully human. Further, the two messages, of necessity, need each other. It is only as people realize what God is like that they have any chance of becoming what they should be like. We often say that people resemble the God, or the gods, whom they worship. To this maxim we might add that, if people have an incorrect view of God, they can never become correct people. This is why the acceptance of Jesus as our example is so vital to the development of Christian character. We learn from Jesus what is right and what is wrong. We learn from Jesus how to forgive sinners, how to have compassion on the afflicted, how to appreciate the lowly, and how to respect women. Jesus' attitude to women is especially important and instructive because He moved among the men and women of His day as a male. In Jesus, we have a picture of true manhood, the kind of manhood for which all other men have been designed.

When Christ was here as man, He dared to identify with a society that was, in many ways, very un-Godlike. There was no perfect world, no ideal society for Him to enter. He accepted the world as He found it. However, He constantly pointed to higher values, He exemplified a nobler humanity, He called women and men to a new loyalty to God's work on earth, that work which He called, "the kingdom of God." Let me present several examples of this upward call of Jesus.

I give these examples from the Gospels as reminders of how Jesus, instead of accommodating Himself to their customs, frequently challenged them to consider radical new ways of thinking and behaving. These examples will, I hope, prepare us to recognize that Jesus was true to His character and calling when He took a profoundly new and different approach in the way He related to women.

The Jews of that day dreamed of political liberation. They longed for the coming of God's promised Messiah to set them free from the indignity of political bondage. In the hills lived fanatical freedom fighters who were ready, as soon as the right leader would emerge, to sacrifice their lives for the sake of national emancipation and the overthrow of the Roman occupation. Jesus, however, revealed no rancor toward the Romans. They also were people whom God loved. One day, a Roman officer approached Jesus, told Him about a sick servant who was in terrible distress, and expressed confidence that Jesus would be able to heal him. Jesus commended him for his faith just as He would have commended a Jew for such faith (Matt. 8:5-13). However, while Jesus Had no word for His fellow Jews on the issue of political freedom, He spoke of the true freedom, which all people needed. This primary freedom would be enjoyed by all those who would accept the truth.

If you continue in my word, you are truly my disciples; and you will know the truth, and the truth will make you free (John 8:31-38).

Jesus met many people who were zealous for the law. He understood them; He endorsed the law Himself. He said He had not come to abolish the law but to fulfill it (Matt. 5:17-20). But then He proceeded to point out the true meaning of the law; He spoke about anger, adultery, divorce, the swearing of oaths, vengeful violence, and the hatred of enemies. Point by point, He challenged them to a higher obedience than they had practiced (Matt. 5:21-48).

The New Manhood of Jesus

Such a view of righteousness they had never understood.

The Jewish people amalgamated their laws and their traditions into a specific culture which they treated as their faith. The vehement denunciations of Jesus, which are listed in Matthew 23, expose the flaws of their system. It was not a system that could honor God and do His will. Repeatedly, Jesus labels them hypocrites. Their piety was only a facade. They were like whitewashed tombs—outwardly attractive but full of dead bones and filth. To their inquiries about law-keeping, Jesus proposed a simple, but profound, alternative: *"Love God with all your heart and soul and mind, and love your neighbor as yourself"* (Matt. 22:34-40).

The Jews had classified all people by value. Both religiously and socially, they knew exactly who was on top and who belonged at the bottom. Jesus, however, ignored such distinctions. Everyone was welcome in His kingdom; anyone was invited to take up the yoke of Jesus. *"Come to me, all you that are weary and are carrying heavy burdens, and I will give you rest"* (Matt. 11:28-30).

In such ways, Jesus turned upside down the established values and norms of His day. He did the same with the prevailing spirit of male supremacy. Jewish rabbis prayed every day, "Blessed art thou, O Lord our God, who hast not made me a woman." Jewish scholars remind us this may not have been as negative as it sounds to our ears. They did not necessarily despise women. Rather, they were grateful for being men because men could study the law and had the opportunity to understand God as women never could. However, the prayer still reminds us of the status of women in that society. Their lives were so restricted that men every day thanked God for the privilege of being male. There was no hint of such a spirit of condescension in the attitudes of Jesus. While His wandering lifestyle required that His band of twelve consist only of men, He never acted as if women were second class. He met them freely and seemed to respect them. He welcomed their ministry to Him and responded graciously and willingly to their needs. The story of Jesus' meeting with the Canaanite woman (Matt. 15:21-28) has sometimes been interpreted as reflecting a derogatory attitude. He acted as if He was reluctant to heal the woman's daughter. However, it seems that Jesus hesitated because He wanted to draw out the full expression of her faith. The delay and extended conversation was probably for the benefit of His disciples. The point is not that she had to prove herself as a woman; she had to prove herself as a Canaanite. Jesus induced her to express her faith clearly and fervently. This was necessary because Jews traditionally regarded Canaanite people as the worst examples of hardness and corruption. What the disciples saw was that even such people could believe and receive then the benefits of Jesus' compassion.

In order to appreciate what an outrageously counter-cultural attitude Jesus took in His relationship with women, we need to recall the details of the previous chapter and try to envision how firmly disrespect for women was entrenched among His peers. To begin with, I must explain that Jesus never fulminated against the strictures their culture had erected against women. He did not denounce the rabbis for their patriarchal attitudes. There is no record of any speech in which Jesus discussed the role of women in society. He uttered no commentary on

The New Manhood of Jesus

gender relationships. He didn't even have a lesson for the twelve about the value of women. However, in contrast to the Greek literature of that era and to the attitude of the Jewish rabbis, the Gospel records allow women to emerge as persons. Jesus treated them as people in their own right. He related to them with respect; He regarded them as fully human. He did not act as if they were morally or intellectually inferior. He gave no hint that they played a secondary role in creation. All four Gospels agree in their witness to this.

While Jesus does not expound on male/female relationships, and while He has no rules about gender roles in the new community of the kingdom, it seems obvious that He is not restricted by the social customs of that day. In His attitudes, His relationships, His occasional pronouncements, and His parables, there are many examples of how His thinking ran contrary to the established ideas of His time. My impression is that Jesus regarded women as fully equal with men and responded to them with an attitude of complete acceptance. This open acceptance is especially significant when the cultural norms and values of that era are considered. His teachings must often have seemed radical; occasionally they must have seemed to disregard recklessly the customs needed to keep life secure and predictable; He must have been watched and heard with fearful uneasiness. It must have seemed to His listeners that He was overturning some of the basic pillars of their society. The prominence in the Gospels of women of faith (especially in Luke) would have been seen by the early readers of the Scriptures as one example of the principle that the last shall be first and the first last. By His teachings and by His actions, Jesus prepared His followers to treat women as full equals in the kingdom of God. Now, if you have not known this Jesus, I invite you to walk with me through the Gospels and meet the most consistent reformer of established gender values of all time.

In this study, it is just as important to notice what Jesus did not say or do as it is to list the details of what He did. As we keep in mind the cultural environment in which He moved, we are impressed by the consistency with which He differed from His peers.

The twelve disciples were men. They were chosen to be with Him, to be witnesses of His ministry, and then to go out as His messengers (Mark 3:14-15). However, there was a larger group of followers who believed in Him and supported Him. In this larger, more informal group, there were women; a few are named specifically (Luke 8:1-3). Mary of Bethany was another such disciple. When Jesus stayed at her family's home, she sat at His feet and listened to His teaching (Luke 10:38-42). In contrast to the social custom which regarded women as incapable of learning and comprehending profound truths, Jesus commended Mary for her desire to be discipled by Him. He was willing to risk public scandal by being seen as a teacher of women. Never in the Gospels is there any indication that Jesus was reluctant about being in the presence of women or conversing with them in public. He gave women the freedom to respond to Him. He dared to dispense with social conventions in order to affirm their humanity and dignity. He was willing to meet and become acquainted with them wherever He encountered them.

The New Manhood of Jesus

We never read that Jesus worked for His own living. In a sense, this is strange. However, since Luke 2:52 says He was obedient to His parents, it is probable that He learned Joseph's trade. Later, He is even referred to as a carpenter (Mark 6:3). However, during His teaching years, He and the disciples seem to have been dependent on others. He received food from the people He visited. No supporting patrons of His work are ever mentioned except a group of female followers, *"who provided for them out of their resources"* (Luke 8:3).

It is significant that Jesus formed direct, personal relationships with women. He did not ask, as we often do today, "Who is your husband?" He did once, though, ask a woman to get her husband (John 4:16). On this occasion, the traveling band had reached the village of Sychar in Samaria. Jesus remained at the well on the outskirts of the town while His disciples went to get some provisions. While Jesus waited, He started a conversation with a woman who had come to draw water. He asked for her husband because He knew she had no husband and He wanted her to admit the sinful relationship in which she lived. When the disciples returned, they were astonished at the freedom which Jesus had to interact with a woman. Their culture saw women as subordinate to men and as functioning in society only through their husbands. It did not seem normal to them for a woman to be visible in public, conversing with a strange man.

This story, in John 4, is actually the most detailed record of any conversation that Jesus had with an individual, and it was with a woman. Further, Jesus revealed to this woman the most important truth about Himself that He ever uttered. He declared to her that He was the Messiah for whom the Jews were waiting. She then became the messenger of good news through which many of her town people came to believe in Jesus.

The law of the Old Testament regarded a woman's periodic menstruations as a ritual uncleanness with which she would contaminate anything she might touch (Lev. 15). Later, Jewish writers seemed obsessed with this uncleanness of women; they saw it as a major reason women were not allowed into the priesthood. However, Jesus was touched by a woman who had been hemorrhaging for twelve years (Luke 8:43-48). He violated Jewish cultural rules by stopping to speak to her. He ignored her uncleanness just as He ignored the uncleanness of lepers and of unwashed food. Instead, He recognized her faith, proclaimed her healed, and pronounced on her His blessing of peace.

The Old Testament has prescriptions for various ceremonial anointings. According to rabbinic teaching, this was always to be done by men. But Jesus, by His consistent attitude of openness to women, created a reputation for acceptance which allowed women to dare to anoint Him. The sinful woman of Luke 7 understood Jesus well enough to approach Him at dinner, weep over His feet, and apply the ointment she had brought. In spite of her bad reputation, Jesus treated her with respect. The Pharisee with whom Jesus was dining looked at Him with contempt. He had no respect for a teacher who would allow himself to be defiled by a disreputable woman from the streets. He concluded that Jesus could not be a prophet as some people had alleged. However, Jesus saw the

The New Manhood of Jesus

occasion as another opportunity to lift a marginalized and downtrodden person out of guilt.

Mary of Bethany anointed Jesus a few days before His crucifixion, and He welcomed that (John 12:1-8). Even though their traditions taught that women had to be kept separate—to sit separately in the synagogues and to visit only their own court in the temple—Jesus allowed them to approach Him and express their feelings in a personal and intimate way.

The healing of the crippled woman, recorded in Luke 13:10-17, is another example of Jesus' clash with the traditions of Judaism over the value of women. A woman came to Him who had been afflicted with a disability for eighteen years. The healing took place on the Sabbath, as Jesus was teaching in the synagogue. The synagogue leader was indignant. However, instead of rebuking Jesus, he berated the woman for her temerity; he reminded her that there were six days each week when she could legitimately come for healing. Jesus, however, would not allow this scolding to go unchallenged. He said to the leader, and all others like him:

> *You hypocrites! Do not each of you on the Sabbath untie his ox or his donkey from the manger and lead it away to give it water? And ought not this woman, a daughter of Abraham whom Satan bound for eighteen long years, be set free from this bondage on the Sabbath day?*

With His response, Jesus implied that the pious men of the day placed greater value on the welfare of their livestock than the health of their women. Jesus came to change such conventions. Women were no longer to be seen as objects men could suppress in their zeal to maintain traditions. They were people too, worthy of the healing grace of God.

Jesus frequently referred to the new community of faith which He had come to establish as the kingdom of God (or "kingdom of heaven" in Matthew's Gospel). It is clear from the beginning that this kingdom is not a men's movement. It is for anyone, regardless of sex, who is willing to submit in faith to God and follow Christ as Lord.

The essence of the kingdom of God is illustrated by the attitude which Jesus took toward His own family. One day, they appeared at the location where He was teaching and requested to see Him (Mark 3:31-35). He did not deny the family ties, but pointed them and all the listeners to the primacy of a new kind of relationship. The basis for entry into the kingdom of God is not a family connection. It is obedience. He turned to the crowd and declared, *"Here are my mother and my brothers! Whoever does the will of God is my brother and sister and mother."* He deliberately made the criterion for admission to the kingdom gender inclusive. Those who do God's will are His brothers and sisters and mothers.

This new faith community was going to function according to entirely new principles. Greatness in the new society would not be based on power or authority, Jesus explains in Luke 22:24-30. Nor would it be based on sexual distinctions. Instead, Jesus teaches, *"The greatest among you must become like the youngest, and the leader like one who serves"* (v. 26). Anyone can be great in the kingdom, anyone, that is, who is willing to follow in the steps of Jesus and be a servant as He was.

I have already referred to the fact that women were primarily valued for their role as child-bearers. When a

The New Manhood of Jesus

woman cried out to Jesus, *"Blessed is the womb that bore you,"* she was speaking as a true daughter of her time. She spoke as a woman who had accepted the fact that the role of a woman was to bear children. Her view was that women served men by producing children for them. She is an example of many women, in different cultures and ages, who have accepted the secondary role of their sex without question. From her perspective, it must have been a joy to have had a child like Jesus. But Jesus corrected her: *"Blessed rather are those who hear the word of God and obey it!"* (Luke 11:27,28). He did not contradict her well-meaning declaration, but pointed her to a higher role, that of obeying and serving God. In the kingdom of God, women are blessed on the same basis as men. Jesus places this equality into its most arresting focus when He declares that prostitutes may enter the kingdom before self-righteous males (Matt. 21:31). He even suggests that a Gentile woman will appear as a valid witness against Jewish men on the day of judgment (Matt. 12:42).

In that day, marriage was seen as normal for all. Women, especially, were seen as severely handicapped if they had to live as singles. However, Jesus saw voluntary singleness and chastity as a valid option (Matt. 19:10-12). By doing so, He opened the door for the participation of women in the missionary outreach of the Church later on.

The society of that day had a deeply ingrained contempt for the moral potential of women; they were seen as small-minded, envious, habitual gossips, dishonest, and unreliable. Jesus, however, entrusted His most significant self-revelations to them. I have already pointed out that the Samaritan woman at the well was the first person to hear His affirmation, "I am he," when she mentioned the coming of the Messiah. As their brother lay dead, Mary and Martha heard the most profound truths about life and death that Jesus ever spoke:

> *I am the resurrection and the life. Those who believe in me, even though they die, will live, and everyone who lives and believes in me will never die. Do you believe this?*

And Martha's response was as clear and emphatic as the disciple Peter's had earlier been: *"Yes, Lord, I believe that you are the Messiah, the Son of God"* (John 11:25,26).

As in other Middle Eastern cultures, Jewish people tended to see women as seductive and as more culpable than men in immoral relationships. However, Jesus treated adultery as equally serious for both sexes (Mark 10:11,12). And when a woman was brought to Him who had been apprehended in the act of adultery, He would not condemn her; rather, He challenged her male accusers to face up to their own sins (John 8:1-11).

Jesus regarded all needy people as worthy of His attention and compassion. He was as concerned over the death of a daughter as over the loss of a son (Matt. 9:18-26; Luke 7:11-17). The disabilities and illnesses of women were treated with the same care and compassion as those of men.

In Jewish culture, women could not serve as witnesses in legal proceedings. They were not considered capable of knowing or speaking the truth. However, Jesus entrusted a group of women, on the morning of His resurrection, with the most important message of all time—the news of His victory over death. Before He revealed Himself to His

The New Manhood of Jesus

male disciples, He commissioned the women to be His witnesses. They had been diligent and faithful all week. The disciples ran in fear when they realized Jesus was in trouble; even Peter lost his courage when he was challenged to admit he was a disciple. And it is important to notice that the Gospel narrators—four men—had accepted enough of the attitude of Jesus and were unbiased enough to report that the women had been more loyal, more trustworthy, and more courageous than the men (Matt. 27:55; Mark 15:40; Luke 23:49; John 20:17). It was this steadfast devotion which brought the women back to the tomb on the first morning of the week. There they heard His announcement, *"I am ascending to my Father..."* (John 20:17).

Jesus welcomed and encouraged women who stepped out of their social positions. He raised them to a higher status than did their society. But more than that, as the Savior of all, He consistently treated them as full equals in the kingdom of God. He now calls on us, those who choose to be His followers, to come and learn from Him (Matt. 11:29). We are to walk in His steps (1 Peter 2:21); we need to think as He thinks and act as He acts to become true children of the Father in heaven. It is Jesus who has demonstrated how God's children are to treat each other.

I suggest that the example of Jesus is so important for the formation of Christian ethics that it should be considered in every moral decision. Years ago, in my student days, I heard Dr. Joseph Fletcher present a lecture on situation ethics. He told of a taxi driver he had met. This man had explained that his father, grandfather, and all other relatives had always voted Republican. Dr. Fletcher had then remarked he assumed the man would follow family tradition and also vote Republican in the approaching federal election. "No, sir," the taxi driver responded. "I'll vote Democrat. Sometimes you just have to break the rules and do what is right." Dr. Fletcher then shouted to the appreciative student audience, "That taxi driver is my hero." I paraphrase that cab driver's philosophy and say, "Sometimes you just have to ignore the customs and do what is right." And doing right always involves the example of Jesus. I realize that the simple question, "What would Jesus do?" does not easily, by itself, solve all ethical dilemmas. Contrary to the hucksters who sell Christian kitsch, wearing a WWJD lapel button may not make much difference in one's life. However, even though this good idea has become a popular slogan, its ultimate relevance has not been negated. If we want to be Christian in our thinking, we have to keep on asking, "What did Jesus do?"

The new manhood of Jesus is not only of historic or academic interest. He is the pattern for the new humanity God wants to establish among all peoples. He was the living example of what it means to be that "new creation" of which the apostle Paul wrote (2 Cor. 5:17). It is a life of new relationships—reconciliation with God, which then makes reconciliation with one another possible.

The Church has historically understood that Jesus is to be our example. The theme of "the imitation of Christ" has been prominent, especially in the more pietistic expressions of Christianity. Many contemporary theologians see the centrality of Jesus Christ as crucial to the correct understanding of the Scriptures. They say we need to take our stand with Him and interpret the Old Testa-

The New Manhood of Jesus

ment from that perspective. Those who do this will often come to the conclusion that violence, militarism, and the worship of the state are to be abjured by the followers of Jesus. They come to this conviction because they interpret the practical significance of the Old Testament from the perspective of Jesus' teachings. Is it too much to expect that they would take the same approach to the letters of the apostles and interpret them in view of how Jesus lived and taught? In other words, should they not accept Jesus' view of women?

The Church of the first century seems to have done so. It is obvious that the New Testament writers had no problem mentioning women as the earliest and most faithful converts (Acts 16:14-15), having charismatic gifts (Acts 21:9), devoted to charity (Acts 9:36-42), dispensing Christian hospitality (Acts 16:15), evangelizing (Rom. 16:3-4; Phil. 4:3), teaching the true meaning of the Christian faith (Acts 18:26), introducing children to faith in God (2 Tim. 1:5), and responsible to guard the Church against error (2 John). Before we pay further attention to the fascinating story of God's work on earth through His people, we must explore what Christ did to make it possible. How did God, in Christ, bring men and women together so that they could actually serve as one in the Church?

Chapter 8

Reconciliation Time

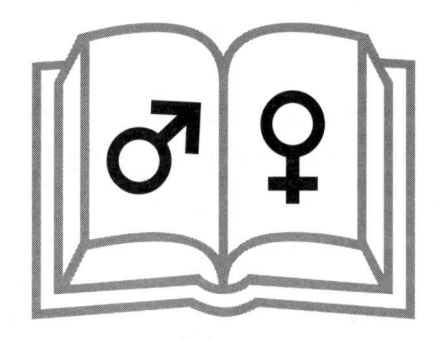

EVERY DAY WE ARE AWARE of the brokenness of the world. All relationships have been damaged by the power of sin. The preview of how it will be is given by God in Genesis 3. Immediately, in the next chapter, comes the first ugly glimpse of how sinful human nature will behave. The oldest son of Adam and Eve murdered his brother, apparently motivated by envy and anger. The chapters that follow describe the development of a primitive civilization. Notable achievements are mentioned. People develop the world which God has given them. But along with the technical progress there is also the growth of violence. The time comes when God sees human wickedness

Reconciliation Time

as so pervasive that the civilization of that era cannot be allowed to continue. While God grants freedom to the people He has made—they can do with their lives and their world whatever they choose—He still rules over them and holds them accountable for what they do with their freedom. He remains God over them. As the sovereign Lord, He responds to their rampant evil (Gen. 6:5-7). So, the world and its achievements are destroyed by the flood.

The new civilization after the flood is not described as violent. The people seem to have lived in unity, but it was a unity in which they agreed to disobey God and rebel against Him. The story is told in Genesis 11. The people agreed to build a tower—likely, a place of worship—that would reach to heaven. Apparently, they saw this as providing them with some kind of security; it was to keep them from being scattered over the whole earth. It also seems to have been an act of disobedience and defiance toward God. However, God confused their language to break up their unholy alliance, and they moved apart. The account of that event is probably meant to show how the many different languages and cultures developed. These differences then led to envy, suspicions, prejudice, extensive conflicts, and the most ruthless wars. Eventually, when by God's choice the descendants of Abraham became a nation among the nations of the world, they had to be part of these counterplots of power, evil, and violence. Except for the occasional interventions of God, they too were subject to the universal law that survival is for the fittest.

The picture of human life in this world, as seen in ancient history, as recorded in the Scriptures, and as reported by the media today, is not attractive. The restlessness in the hearts of people and the turbulence among the nations is evidence of the destructive powers of sin. The prejudice and conflicts among the various ethnic groups, between blacks and whites, between the sexes, between rich and poor, among the disciples of conflicting political ideologies, and among the zealots of different religious confessions, keep on reminding us that human life is not as it ought to be. People have left God and lost His peace. They are at enmity with God and, consequently, have lost the ability to be at peace among themselves.

But God has not abandoned the world to its painful corruptions. He never intended to. The curses of Genesis 3 and the preview of the resultant human misery were not His last words. From the beginning, God planned to bring peace to His troubled people. God would take on physical form and introduce His grace to the world. And all of creation would be invited to return to obedience, the harmony and the peaceful order from which it had strayed.

The Scriptures declare that Jesus Christ, the eternal Son, died for sin. In Him, God made peace with the world. By receiving Him, the people of the world may not only find peace with God but also peace with themselves. In Christ, the pervasive and destructive effects of the original rebellion and the continuing arrogance and attempted autonomy of ruined humankind can be healed. From the beginning, Jesus was called the Savior. He came to make right what people for thousands of years had done wrong. The New Testament calls it reconciliation.

All this is from God, who reconciled us to himself through Christ, and has given us the ministry of

Reconciliation Time

reconciliation; that is, in Christ God was reconciling the world to himself, not counting their trespasses against them, and entrusting the message of reconciliation to us (2 Cor. 5:18-21).

On the one hand, it was making peace with God. On the other hand, it opened the possibility for the healing of rifts among people. By virtue of their faith-union with Jesus Christ, separated people can now come together and be one.

The vision of the ideal new humankind that Christ came to create is perhaps best expounded in Paul's letter to the new Galatian believers. The letter was written because Paul had heard that some teachers in Galatia were trying to enforce the Jewish rite of circumcision in the Church. The apostle was incensed. He pronounced this teaching to be heresy; he saw it as divisive and destructive. He declared that if they practiced the rite of circumcision, they separated themselves from Christ; Christ could be of no help to them (Gal. 5:2-4). In the earlier chapters of the letter, he had explained his convictions. The starting point of his argument was God's promise to Abraham. That promise was already seen as leading, in some way, to blessing for all people, not just the physical descendants of Abraham. That covenant with Abraham had now been fulfilled in Jesus Christ. All of the Old Testament law was preparatory, looking ahead to the day when God would do what He had promised. Now, that ancient blessing had arrived. And what are the details of that blessing? It is that all people can be children of God through faith.

> *For in Christ Jesus you are all children of God through faith. As many of you as were baptized into Christ have clothed yourselves with Christ. There is no longer Jew or Greek, there is no longer slave or free, there is no longer male or female; for all of you are one in Christ Jesus.*

This passage expresses the very essence of the Gospel. This is what it means to be in Christ. The repetitions, as with powerful hammer strokes, drive home the universalism which must be true of the Christian Church.

I will treat this passage as the basis for my development of the theme of reconciliation. Three sets of deeply divided classes are mentioned here: 1) Jews and Greeks; 2) slaves and free; 3) males and females. Through their incorporation into Jesus Christ, all these polarized people may become one. The main objective of the letter to the Galatians is to show that attempts to perpetuate the traditional societal divisions are contrary to the Gospel message; they are obstructions to God's will, and they nullify Christ's reconciling work. Earlier, I referred to the prayer which a Jewish man would regularly pray, thanking God he had not been created as a Gentile, a slave, or a woman. It almost seems as if the three sets of antitheses were chosen deliberately because of the three-fold privilege for which pious Jewish males thanked God. It seems that Paul made a bold and intentional thrust to turn upside down an important aspect of the Jewish value system.

The first of the three divisions listed in Galatians 3, receives the most urgent attention in the Scriptures. It seems that, to begin with, even Jesus' disciples did not

Reconciliation Time

understand God's will on this issue. When Jesus said that they would be His witnesses to the ends of the world they, apparently, thought of this as sharing Christ with Jewish people everywhere. The first major breakthrough in this restricted thinking came when Peter changed his mind. He received a definite divine message that he was to preach in the house of Cornelius, a Roman officer. When he did so, the entire household was awakened to the faith and received baptism. Later, when he explained the specifics of the divine call and the results of his obedience to his critical colleagues in Jerusalem, they exclaimed, *"Then God has given even to Gentiles the repentance that leads to life"* (Acts 11:18).

That burst of insight, however, did not solve all problems; in fact, it immediately created new difficulties for the Church. If Jews and Gentiles could both be called Christians and belong to the same Church, by whose moral principles would they live? That question necessitated the first major gathering of Church leaders, as described in Acts 15. After an extensive consultation, they agreed that, even though the Church had begun with Jewish believers, the Gentiles who were now receiving Christ did not need to become Jews to be one with them. They received a new vision of the direction in which God was leading His Church and they attributed this insight to the guidance of the Spirit (Acts 15:28). In any case, Paul explains, in Galatians 2, that he had already argued earlier that Gentile believers were free from the obligations of the law.

The apostle, with the entire council in Jerusalem, recognized that, unless the Jewish and the Gentile believers could accept each other as equals and live together in

Christ, the Church could not truly represent God's reconciling work. Racial segregation would be a denial of the gospel. Compelling the Gentile to become a Jew would be a contradiction of God's way of redemption. The letter to the Galatian churches deals primarily with this racial/religious issue; if they impose the regulations of Old Testament law on Gentile believers, they deny their conversion (3:1-4).

It remained for Paul, in his later letter to the Ephesians, to develop the most systematic statement of the unity created by the sacrifice of Christ (2:11-22). He explains that the Jews, who used to think of themselves as close to God, and the Gentiles who seemed to be far away, have been brought together by Christ. The dividing wall has been broken down. In Jesus Christ, there is peace between the people who were formerly separated. Through Him, God created one new humanity. Those who once were strangers and aliens are now fellow citizens. Consequently, there is only one Church being built upon the one foundation. As a result of this unifying work of Christ, they are now called to maintain and live in the unity they have in the Spirit (4:3). Spiritual unity is not only a theory; it is meant to be lived out in the Church.

The unifying work God has done on earth is also mentioned in the letter to the Colossian believers. The language is different, but the underlying theme is the same. Again, God is seen as having created a new community out of the many disparate peoples.

In that renewal there is no longer Greek and Jew, circumcised and uncircumcised, barbarian, Scythian, slave and free; but Christ is all and in all! (3:10-11).

Reconciliation Time

This new coherence, says the writer, is designed according to the image of the Creator. The symbol of this new unity, defined in these letters to the young churches, is baptism (Col. 2:12). As I explained above, the occasion for Paul's letter to the Galatians was the question whether or not believers needed to be circumcised in order to be true members of the Church. Circumcision, in the Old Testament, was specifically a male rite. It identified Jewish males as belonging to God's covenant. In contrast to the former ritual, baptism is for all, females as well as males, Gentiles as well as Jews. Every baptism service in the early Church would have been a reminder that the traditional distinctions which formerly served as the basis for social structuring had been erased.

It is obvious that, of the three sets of polarities mentioned in Galatians 3:28, the second and the third do not receive as much direct attention in the Scriptures as the first. Apparently, the division between Jews and Gentiles, which existed primarily in the minds of the Jews, was so fundamentally contrary to the essence of what it means to be the Church that no effort was spared to correct it. It should be remembered here that the Jewish concept of superiority and exclusiveness came out of God's dealings with them in the past. They thought they had been divinely chosen to be first among the peoples of the world. They had been called to be God's people; the Gentile nations had not received that same call. They could have argued that, if they were prejudiced, their prejudices were based upon God's election. The word of the Lord had always come to them through Hebrew speakers in Hebrew words. Similar arguments have been presented by those who have wished to defend the other two divisions that Paul mentions. Not long ago, some white Christians devoutly believed they had been designated, by creation, to have a superior role over blacks. Today, many Christians still scour the Bible for arguments to bolster their feeling that women should be subordinate to men. Once a custom or a tradition is entrenched in society, it cannot easily be vanquished. However, in the first century, the apostles of grace and freedom won their case. The Spirit was victorious. Gentile and Jewish believers could belong to one Church. The traditions were superceded and the Church kept on spreading as one body.

The societal division between slaves and free people gets a different treatment. Apparently, slave and master could function side by side in the same Church (Col. 3:22-24; 1 Tim. 6:1-3; Philemon 16). No New Testament writers directly challenge the strongly established convention of slavery in the Roman Empire. However, they teach both, slaves and masters, to respect each other as fellow Christians and to treat each other with Christian grace. This does not mean that it is right, or that it ever has been right, for one person to own another as his property. Even though the principle of human equality was clearly declared in Galatians, Ephesians, and Colossians, it was only in the nineteenth century that Western Christians could finally get themselves to face the social implications of this doctrine. Old traditions die hard.

Most Christians today are deeply distressed by the frequent reports of slavery and abuse of minority rights in different countries. They now understand that any discrimination on the basis of rank, ethnicity, or color is an affront to human dignity and a violation of the plan of the

Reconciliation Time

Creator. That European and North American governments frequently express concern over violation of human rights in other nations, may often sound rather paternalistic, but it is still evidence of how extensively New Testament values have permeated even secular thinking.

The fact that the New Testament never demands Christians not to own slaves, agrees with a principle noted here earlier; God can accept and work through people who do not yet understand His will. That, however, does not mean that they may relax and leave matters as they are. The cross of Jesus Christ is always before us, beckoning us upward, inviting us to step out of the past and dare to live by the new principles of His kingdom.

The polarity between men and women is treated likewise, not with any ambivalence, but with patience. The principle of equality in Christ is emphatically pronounced, but the practical outworking of that, it seems, was left to time. Slavery would naturally become intolerable once masters and slaves regarded each other as fellow Christians. It still surprises me that it took so long. (In fact, we, in our developed countries, need to confess that the ideal of human equality is not yet being applied consistently, right at home, in our relationships with the minority groups who live in our midst. Old traditions die hard.) The polarity between men and women, on the other hand, would be erased once people recognized the way of the Spirit among God's people. And again I am surprised it has taken until this century for the implications of Pentecost to start sinking in.

I need to respond to the idea that being one in Christ, as Galatians 3:28 puts it, is only a spiritual quality and not a functional responsibility. It has been argued that this statement, and others like it, speak only of our relationship to God and not of our life together in the Church. With respect to the male/female issue, this argument says they are equally saved in Christ, but they need not be treated as equals in the Church. I listen to this argument and wonder, do we think Paul would have intended this type of distinction for the first two sets of polarities? Do we imagine he could have meant that Jews and Greeks have equal value before God, but Church leaders have to be Jews? While racial distinctions keep on being made in the Church, sometimes formally, sometimes informally, we agree that such discriminations are contrary to the principle of this text. Usually differentiations such as these are a matter of unspoken policy (and even those prejudices we would be ashamed to admit have a stubborn way of enduring).

It has also been pointed out, quite correctly I believe, that the line, "all of you are one," does not refer primarily to equality, but to unity. Paul is arguing that, in spite of the traditional societal divisions there can be only one Church. He has first of all asserted that "there is no longer Jew or Greek, there is no longer slave or free, there is no longer male and female." This statement seems to say that the significant differences have been erased. It does not mean that the distinctions do not exist anymore but that they don't matter now. There is an equality among those who have clothed themselves with Christ. And this equality is a real and meaningful fact because of the unity these people have in Christ Jesus, "for all of you are one." The consequence of the unity is that being male or female makes no difference in the Church.

Reconciliation Time

I wonder how we can demonstrate the validity of a deep spiritual truth, if we are not willing to put it into visible practice. Shouldn't the equality of women and men be a noticeable feature of every congregation? Shouldn't it show? Halford Luccock, a respected American minister of a few generations back, compared the message of Galatians 3:28 to a great drama rehearsed behind closed doors. To this analogy, I add that sections of it have already been previewed by the public. What has been seen has been acclaimed as very good. However, the great divine drama of full reconciliation between all peoples still waits for complete public performance. Isn't it time the Christian Church present the entire drama to the world?

Sociological studies are frequently being done on the lives of the oppressed and disenfranchised. Maybe it's time to ask some questions of those who have the power to be in control. What is the desperate feeling of inferiority which has driven white people to shout to the whole world that their skin color earns them an advantage over all other humans? What is the source of the pervasive fear which compels the rich and the powerful to keep asserting supremacy over the poor and the weak? What do we make of the arrogance which inspires men to claim that, simply because they are male, they are superior to females? Is this a mark of valor and resoluteness, or is it infantile weakness?

The fracture between Jew and Gentile was brought to the cross of Christ and there it was healed. In later centuries, though, whenever the Church moved from its grounding in the reconciling Gospel, old prejudices and hostilities emerged again. The Church has not had a good record of dealing with its latent anti-Semitism. The division between the black slave people and the white free people is still in the process of being reconciled. Do we now dare, after all these years, to recognize that there is another venerable social division that needs the healing touch of Christ's redemptive love? Can we admit that it is a sin to treat women as second-rate? Can we admit that just as Jewish Christians once put down Gentile believers and Christian churches despised Jews, just as powerful white people defended their right to subordinate blacks, so men have traditionally treated women as if the reconciling work of Jesus makes no difference to this relationship? Or will we continue to deny the existence of the problem? Denial is always a barrier to understanding and reconciliation and healing. Can we do it? It will mean that we will have to recognize wholeheartedly the lordship of Jesus Christ over His Church. And we will have to become willing to submit to the ministry of the Spirit in the Church.

Chapter 9

And Then the Spirit Came

THE PROPHETS OF THE Old Testament had a constant message of challenge—repent, submit to the laws of God, give up your stubborn willfulness, let go of your hardness, and change your ways. While the prophets exposed sin, they also preached grace. Alongside the message of condemnation, there were promises of restoration; together with the theme of despair, there were notes of hope. The prophets believed that a better and a holier life was possible, but they were constantly distressed by the tragic moral weakness they saw even among those who professed to know God. The law offered the people God's blessings and a good life. But they kept on following sinful instincts and brought upon themselves sorrows and troubles which always accompany disobedience.

Then, occasionally, as if by a quantum leap, the prophets saw visions of a glorious new era in the future. They saw a time when God would do a new thing on earth. They saw a people transformed by the grace of God and serving Him with power and joy. It is not always clear how these visions are to be interpreted. Are they exalted and figurative images of an immediate national renewal and political restoration? Sometimes it seems so. In other cases, these visions seem to refer to the new age of the Spirit to be inaugurated by the action of God at some point in the future.

In some cases, the New Testament helps us with the meaning of these triumphant visions. The promise of a new covenant in Jeremiah 31:33-34 is interpreted in Hebrews 8 as predicting the covenant which God would make with the world through the sacrificial death of Christ. The passage in Hosea 1:10, about the new people who will become the children of God, is treated, in Romans 9:26, as referring to the Gentiles who will enter the kingdom of Christ. There are other texts that look ahead to a major turning point in God's way of dealing with the intransigent perversity of people. For our purposes, the most important is Joel 2:28-29. In the same vein as in the passages cited above, the prophet Joel speaks for God and says:

> *Then afterward I will pour out my spirit on all flesh; your sons and your daughters shall prophecy, your old men shall dream dreams, and your young men shall see visions. Even on the male and female slaves, in those days, I will pour out my spirit.*

And Then the Spirit Came

After the resurrection of Jesus, the disciples remained together in Jerusalem. They had seen Christ ascend and understood they would not see Him anymore. Further, they knew it was up to them to proclaim the story of Christ throughout the world (Acts 1:8). They also knew this task would require power they did not have. So they were waiting for the Spirit, whom Jesus had promised, to come upon them. Jesus told them the Spirit would empower them for their worldwide witness.

On the fiftieth day after the resurrection, it happened. While they were worshiping, the Spirit of God was given to them. The assembly consisted of women and men (Acts 1:14). And the account in Acts 2 stresses the fact that the entire assembly of believers received the Spirit on this occasion. *"They were all together in one place"* (v.1) and then *"all of them were filled with the Holy Spirit and began to speak in other languages, as the Spirit gave them ability"* (v.4). The visitors to Jerusalem heard them praising God in the different languages of the home communities from which they had come. I regard this miraculous experience as a symbolic affirmation of the vision Jesus had for His Church. He had declared that they would be His witnesses to the ends of the earth. They were now reminded that, by the empowering presence of the Spirit, it would be possible. And we must assume that all of them, the disciples, the other believers, and the women, were participating in this new experience of Spirit-given speech. When the astonished crowd interpreted this as a case of early morning drunkenness, Peter explained that these signs were effected by the Spirit and this unusual phenomenon was exactly what the prophet Joel had predicted.

As Peter understood it, this prophetic speaking of men and women was a sign of the new age of the Spirit which the ascended Christ was now inaugurating. What the Spirit-filled Christ had begun in person would be continued by Spirit-filled men and women. The anointed speaking of these women and men was regarded as a fulfillment of the prophecy God had spoken through Joel. After this Pentecostal experience, it would have been incongruous if the disciples had forbidden women to engage in public preaching. The equal equipping of women and men for public ministry was the initial sign that this movement was God's doing.

It is important to recall that, in the Old Testament era, the Holy Spirit already moved among God's people. One person here, another there, was gifted and blessed by the Spirit for special service (Exod. 31:3-5; Num. 11:29; Judg. 3:10). It was an experience, however, which is only rarely mentioned. Now, as Joel had predicted and Peter interpreted, the Spirit came upon all flesh (Acts 2:14-21). All were filled with the presence of God. Both sons and daughters would prophesy. Both young and old would have visions and dreams. Even the slaves, both male and female, would be filled with the Spirit and speak God's message.

So Pentecost (the day the Spirit was poured out on all believers) must be seen as the big turning point. God embarked on a new way of operating in His world. For thousands of years, women had been ignored; often they had been despised, mistreated, and abused. For thousands of years, God had waited while sin worked out its havoc in human relationships. But now, God was declaring a new beginning. The power of evil had been shattered

And Then the Spirit Came

by the death of Jesus on the cross. Now the Spirit was poured out to change the hearts of people; the mission of the Spirit would be to transform human relationships throughout society, putting into effect the redemption that had been procured for all. The Spirit came upon all believers. All were empowered—men and women, slaves and free, Jews and Gentiles. In the future, the freedom of women might still be limited by the sanctions of culture, but there was no longer any question about God's will. That women and men are equal before Him was confirmed when the Spirit came.

The Pentecost event is one of the most important steps in God's program for redeeming the world. It is the key to understanding how God plans to work through His Church. The Church is the body of Christ, meaning, it belongs to Christ. This is true, not only because He died for it, but because He, as Spirit, now lives within it. The indwelling Spirit of Christ gives direction to the Church, provided the Church is willing to be directed by Him. The Spirit produces within the individual believers the graces and virtues necessary for a convincing witness. From Him comes the power, the enthusiasm, and the joy to be a witness for Jesus in a tough, dangerous, discouraging world. Further, the Spirit keeps on holding before the Church the big vision of God, that the whole world is to be introduced to the Savior, Jesus Christ.

In my opinion, the coming of the Holy Spirit clinches the case I have been developing since chapter 5. Over the years, as I reflected on the restrictions the New Testament seems to place on the ministry of women (these texts will be discussed in chapter 11), I couldn't deny or discard the implications of this pivotal event at Pentecost. I came to the conclusion that, if I wanted to honor God and show respect for His gracious work of world redemption, I could not ignore what Pentecost had to say about the work of both women and men in the Church of Jesus Christ.

The Jewish people thought of God as living in the temple in Jerusalem. He was at home behind the curtain, in the Holy of Holies, where no common person could ever go. God had His place apart from the people. When Jesus died, that venerable concept was shattered with a dramatic, symbolic, heavenly act. The curtain in the temple, that restraint which kept the ministering priests from looking into dwelling place of God, was torn from top to bottom (Matt. 27:51). The complement to the opening of the Holy of Holies was the Pentecostal pouring out of the Spirit of God upon the disciples in Jerusalem. God would be at home in all of His people. Christians since then have still built impressive cathedrals, abbeys, and churches to remind worshippers of the greatness of God. Sometimes, these awesome sanctuaries have been regarded as special holy places. However, the New Testament teaching about the coming of the Holy Spirit reminds us that we have no holy places; we only have holy people. The apostle Paul spoke to a congregation when he asked, *"Do you not know that you are God's temple and that God's Spirit dwells in you?"* (1 Cor. 3:16). Later, he directed his attention to the individual believer and asked again:

> *Do you not know that your body is a temple of the Holy Spirit within you, which you have from God, and that you are not your own?* (1 Cor. 6:20).

In neither case, whether addressing the Church body or the individual believer, is there a hint of any distinction between the male and female members of the Church.

One of the functions of the Spirit is to change people, to transform their morals and enlighten their minds with heavenly wisdom. As an example of such a spiritual transformation, I choose the man we know as Paul. He was a product of the strictest Judaism, a Pharisee, a Hebrew of the Hebrews, a zealous defender of Hebrew traditions and blameless as far as the requirements of the law were concerned (Phil. 3:5-6). He was probably a bachelor or a widower; at least, he never mentions a woman in his life. He actually explains that he did not have a wife as his companion on his preaching trips as some of the other apostles did (1 Cor. 9:5). In his early days, as he attempted to exterminate the Church of Jesus, he made no distinction between men and women; whoever professed faith in Jesus was dragged off to prison (Acts 8:3). By the way, the fact that women were arrested along with men in the early days of the Church, is evidence of their prominence. By their full involvement in the life of the Church, they lost the protected status women have often had in strictly patriarchal societies. Later, when Paul was transformed into a follower of Jesus, he showed the same disregard for the difference between women and men. As I detailed in chapter 6, he could accept both women and men as his fellow witnesses. In contrast to the usual attitude of ancient people toward women, he regarded them with deep respect. Earlier, both Christian men and Christian women had been his enemies; now, both were his fellow workers in the faith. In view of how difficult it is for men to change their minds—I know all about it—this change in Paul is as remarkable as his change from persecutor of the Church to its most outspoken proponent.

Another purpose of the Spirit was to guide and inspire the writers who recorded the events of Jesus and the early Church. As an example of such a Spirit-guided apostle, I use Luke. He is the author of the gospel according to Luke and of the Acts of the Apostles. Of the four Gospel witnesses, he was the most cosmopolitan in his outlook and interests. If I may use the word in this context, I would say he is the most "worldly" of the four. Various hints in his material suggest that he was probably not a Jew but a Greek. This Luke, inspired by the Spirit, looks beyond the common utilitarian view which Greek people had of their women and recognizes their full humanity in Christ. Scholars have often noted that, as he researches the events on which he wants to report (Luke 1:1-3), he has a special eye for the qualities and contributions of women.

To begin with, there is the contrast between Zacharias and Mary in the first two chapters of his Gospel. Luke is the only witness to present these details. Zacharias was elderly, a religious leader, a man. But he doubted the word of God which the angel brought to him and turned dumb. Mary was young, presumably poor, and a woman. The message that came to her was as incredible as that which Zacharias heard, but she believed and added her "yes" to the heavenly announcement.

Luke is the only one to report on the contrast between the sinful woman who washed Jesus' feet with her tears and the self-righteous Pharisee who criticized her devotion (Luke 7:36-50). It is also Luke who writes about the

And Then the Spirit Came

crippled woman who came to Jesus for healing and the synagogue leader who reminded her sternly that she could have come on the six days when it would have been lawful to be healed, not on the Sabbath (Luke 13:10-17). It seemed natural for the disciples to speak of *"some women of our group"* (Luke 24:22) and for Luke to report it. Throughout Acts, women are readily mentioned as responding to the new faith and being active in the Church. There is no reticence about citing them. Secular historians have often been accused of overlooking the role of women in society; biblical historians cannot be accused of the same. My explanation for this is that the Spirit's influence overruled their innate male biases.

The most significant aspect of the Spirit's influence, however, is the equipping of all believers for their service. The Church of Jesus Christ is now the agency through which the Spirit works in the world. For this ministry, the members of the Church receive specific spiritual gifts. Three New Testament passages discuss these gifts: Romans 12:3-8; 1 Corinthians 12-14; 1 Peter 4:10-11. The meaning of a gift is never formally given. However, each of the gifts mentioned has to do with serving others in the Church. God works through His people; to equip them as His servants, spiritual gifts are given. The purpose always is to build up the Church. When everyone uses her or his gift, the Church will become healthy, strong, and will keep growing (Eph. 4:11-16). Since every member receives a gift, every one is to be involved in this work of building (1 Cor. 12:7). The designation of the gifts—who gets which gift for which service—is the Spirit's choice (1 Cor. 12:11). While all believers are gifted for service, there is a wide variation in the types of gifts they have. It is an important concern of the apostle that these variations in giftedness would not be a schismatic factor in the Church. Rather, 1 Corinthians 12-14 teaches that the variety is a source of strength and enrichment; there is a fullness in the diversity.

The believers in Corinth seem to have been excited about the new gifts they experienced. However, in the newness of their faith, they misunderstood their purpose. They were proud of their new abilities and seem to have flaunted them as personal glories. They were eager to put themselves on public display. Paul accuses them of having boasted about their gifts (1 Cor. 4:7). He teaches that the gifts were not given to expand their own egos but were bestowed upon them for the purpose of building up and encouraging the Church. When the question about the value of a particular gift arises, the criterion must always be, "Does it build the Church?" (1 Cor. 14:1-5).

Since spiritual gifts are intended to be used, their neglect or suppression would mean impoverishment for the Church. The ministry of gifted people is discussed in Ephesians 4:11-16. The concluding point is that each member of the Church has to be serving appropriately in order for the whole Church to grow toward maturity. To sum up, the Scriptures teach that all believers have been equipped by the Spirit, and when every person is using his or her gift, the Church will be a healthy community. All this leads to this inevitable conclusion: if God works in His Church through people whom He has empowered for such ministry, forbidding anyone to use a gift seems like an insult to God. It would seem to say that we know better than God. Further, such a restriction would sentence the Church to an

And Then the Spirit Came

existence below its full potential. It would mean that some gifts lie unused, some spiritual resources are wasted. Yet the Church has, by tradition and sometimes by official policy, restricted women from certain ministries without paying regard to the gifts they may have received from God.

There is no indication anywhere that certain gifts are only for men and other gifts are specifically for women. There is no suggestion that gifts will be granted on an equally proportionate basis either. Someone might argue that certain gifts will never be given to women. To that, we can only say that it is the Holy Spirit who decides who gets which gift. There seems to be some sequence in the importance of gifts: *"God has appointed in the church first apostles, second prophets, third teachers; then..."* (1 Cor. 12:28). It is never said that men would receive the gifts at the top of the list and that the lower gifts are for women. In fact, prophecy is second from the top and the early Church accepted the ministry of women who spoke prophecy (Acts 21:9; 1 Cor. 11:5). At Pentecost, the prophecy of Joel was recalled: *"your sons and your daughters shall prophecy"* (Acts 2:17). That practice continued as the Church spread into the world with its witness.

At this point, it seems appropriate to raise the question: Who discerns which gift a person does have? If the gifts are as important as the paragraphs above have argued, the discernment of gifts becomes a matter of high priority in the Church. Who will be assigned, or allowed, to practice which ministry in the Church? The answer must be that the recognition of the gift will happen in the circle or in the community in which the gifted person serves. It can only be done by those who are present to notice the effects of the ministry and are close enough to know the motives and attitudes of the person being observed. This is how it has always been. The Israelites of the Old Testament heard various prophets. Sometimes, different prophets contradicted each other (e.g. Jer. 29). One prophet would accuse another of speaking falsehoods. In such cases, it was logically not possible that both could be speaking for the Lord. It was the people, through the working of the Spirit in their hearts, who recognized which prophet was of the Lord. In this present era of the Spirit, it is those who are spiritual who can recognize spiritual truth (1 Cor. 2). God has gifted the Church for this process of discerning (1 Cor. 12:10). In worship services, as Paul explains, it is the people who listen who are expected to discern whether or not the speaker's words are of the Lord (1 Cor. 14:29). The apostle John sees such spiritual testing as essential to protect the Church against false teachings (1 John 4:1-3). Throughout the story of the Church in the New Testament, it was this Spirit-given authority that was used to choose people for ministry (Acts 6; 1 Tim. 1:18; 2 Tim. 1:6). It is in the community of the Spirit that spiritual gifts are recognized. And the gifts are recognized, not by evaluating training or intellectual credentials or by following administrative policies, but by asking, "What is God doing in our midst through this person?"

We often speak in our church communities about "the call." By this, we mean that God, the sovereign Lord of the Church, calls people to specific ministries. There have been questions and controversies about the form and meaning of such a call. Since all believers have now been

And Then the Spirit Came

endowed with the Spirit, people have wondered if "the call" is still a legitimate concept. This study of the Spirit's role in the Church leads me to declare that, yes, God still calls people to serve. He calls to a specific ministry by granting the gift for that work. This seems to be an inevitable consequence of the New Testament's teaching on spiritual gifts. Gifts are meant to be used. Gifts are given by God. So those who have been gifted have been called by God.

This leads me to wonder: How can we say to God, "This woman, whom you have blessed with a beautiful and gracious spirit and who has been remarkably endowed with a gift for ministry, must not use her gift in our church"? Isn't such a stance a rejection of the work of God? And can we expect God to bless a church which prays for gifted people and then refuses to accept the ministry of those He has equipped?

I conclude this section by noting that the biblical theme of equality rests upon three pivotal divine events. First, men and women were created equal. Second, they were redeemed to be equal. Third, they were confirmed in their equality at Pentecost. Further, I point out that this simple formula for the principle of equality is also rooted in the doctrine of the Trinity. First, we speak of God as the Creator; He is the God above us who created men and women as equals. Second, we know God as the Redeemer; He is the God beside us who gave His life to redeem us from the sins that separate us. Third, we believe in God the Spirit; He is the God within us who indwells and empowers us equally, whether we are male or female.

Chapter 10

So Now There Should Be Equality

EVEN THOUGH THE BIBLICAL case for equality seems clear enough to be understood by all those who are willing to consider the idea, equality has had a spotty history in the Church. From early Church records we learn that the vision of the apostles began to fade after the first century. As the anticipation of the imminence of the kingdom gave way to the practical task of fitting into the cultural customs of the day and co-existing with the societies around them, the Church slowly began to resemble the world out of which it had been called. They inherited, out of the first century, both the doctrine of oneness in Christ and the social convention of the subordination of

So Now There Should Be Equality

women. As it often does, the cultural practice won out over the theological principle.

However, in spite of the long history of human compromise and inconsistency, the Holy Scriptures continue to call all men and women to respect each other as equals. The Church has not been a total failure on this issue. Christians have, in many respects, been the salt of the earth. Consequently, some of the principles I will list below have been accepted and taken for granted, even by secular societies. To help us see the total picture of equality as the New Testament has it, I list here both the points on which people have generally agreed as well as points that are still debated. In the Church of Jesus Christ, in that new order in which men and women have been reconciled to each other and to God, the following aspects of equality should be recognized and put into practice.

Women and men are equal in their marital sexual partnership (1 Cor. 7:1-6). They have equal privileges and responsibilities toward each other. The rights and authority of the husband and wife are identical. Both are asked to defer to each other and to consider each other's needs.

They are equally responsible for their sins. The account of Ananias and Sapphira, in Acts 5, illustrates this principle. The wife was just as responsible for their dishonest scheme as the husband. There is no basis in Scripture for the notion that women are more saintly than men, nor for the idea that women, in their weakness, can hide behind their husbands in sinning. There are sinners and saints of both sexes.

They are equally free to make their own faith commitments to Christ. While the decision to follow Christ was sometimes a family matter (Acts 16:33), it is assumed that there will be, in the Church, both men and women whose spouses are not believers (1 Cor. 7:13-14; 1 Peter 3:1-7). Nowhere is there any suggestion that women are dependent upon men for faith, or that they have to wait for men to take the leadership in accepting Christ, or that they need to ask for the approval of men before they can commit themselves to faith.

Women and men, by virtue of their faith, are equally "in Christ." In spite of some equivocation about the meaning of 1 Timothy 2:15 (that verse, which can be read as teaching that women are saved through bearing children, will be discussed in the next chapter), most Christians agree that both are saved by grace. Together we are *"heirs of the gracious gift of life"* (1 Peter 3:7).

Men and women are equally responsible to live disciplined and virtuous lives in Christ. In Philippians 2:2, Paul admonishes the whole Church to be in agreement and live in harmony. Then, in 4:2, that counsel is directly applied to two women. They are specifically singled out; they too had to learn to be of the same mind in the Lord.

Both sexes have the privilege of being filled with the Holy Spirit when they submit themselves to Jesus Christ in faith (Acts 2). The Spirit of God is gender blind. Women and men have the same spiritual benefits, that of being guided, inspired, and empowered for their life of service in Christ.

They are equal in their access to the Church of Jesus Christ. The terms used in the New Testament to identify the people of the church—"saints," "servants," "disciples," and "brothers"—are applied equally to male and female believers.

So Now There Should Be Equality

Women and men are equally acceptable for the service for which they are gifted. The New Testament discusses spiritual giftedness without any reference to gender qualifications. There is never a suggestion that a gift may be restricted to one sex or another. They were equally appreciated and recognized by the apostle Paul for their ministry, as is seen in Romans 16. He did not even list the men first and then the women, as later Christians have done. Nor did he identify any of the women by the men to whom they may have been married. Each person, whether male or female, received his or her personal word of commendation.

They are of equal significance and value in God's redemptive program. Female converts are mentioned specifically, sometimes by name (Acts 17:4,34). The gospel appealed to women, and to have women respond to a preaching mission was seen as worthy of mention.

After having listed the ways in which men and women are equal before God, I must now note that equality is not sameness. The New Testament does not deny gender distinctives. We have distinctly sexed bodies, but we are equal as humans in God's redeemed order. We must discard the idea that there is a primary or dominant sex. Just as we must not hold to the idea that whites are superior to blacks, that rich people have more value to God than poor people, or that educated people are more human that illiterates, so we must not cling to the view that males are superior to females. The subordination of women, as if they are merely secondary, is wrong. To reduce the status of women so that they are seen as mere adjuncts to men, whether sexually, domestically, or professionally, is sinful. Such unjust demotions are a denial of God's plan for creation, a denial of the redemptive work of Christ, and a denial of the Holy Spirit who works through both women and men.

Women are just as important in the community of Jesus as are men. They also can love God, commit themselves to live for Christ, and submit their wills in obedience to the Spirit who dwells within them (I'm actually embarrassed to mention these obvious details; I do so only because I have heard men talk as if women are so weak they cannot be expected to measure up to the high model of male religious devotion). Consequently, in setting Church policy, in directing the life of the Church, in planning the ministry of the Church, their insight and opinions are just as important as men's.

I am not arguing that we should indiscriminately legislate women into positions of leadership. Rather, I am making a plea for opening our churches to the work of the Spirit. We need to confront the traditions that oppose such an openness. The Church needs to be released from the bondage of restrictive traditions so it can again reflect God's creative plan that women and men are to work as co-servants in their stewardship over God's world.

When we assign people to ministries in the church, we must remember we are acting for Jesus Christ, the Lord of the Church. His call to service is not based on gender. We have seen that in the Old Testament as well as the New, God would bypass human ordinances and call women to serve Him. His call is based on giftedness. Those He has endowed for service are called by Him to serve.

When a church sets up restrictions to keep women out of ministry roles, it is depriving itself of the contributions

So Now There Should Be Equality

of half of its people. This seems terribly unfortunate, since God has created the sexes to compliment each other as they work together. In the home, in society at large, and in the Church, men and women should respect each other, treat each other as equals, and accept thankfully the contributions which both sexes can make to the life of the community. It is difficult to see how the Church would not be enriched immensely and become more Godlike if both sexes were encouraged to participate fully in its life.

Now the question has to be faced: Can we be faithful to the doctrine of equality if we agree that men and women are of equal value before God but then insist they must have distinct and different roles in the Church? Is the concept "equality in being but difference in function" a valid and biblical idea? Or does it contradict itself? I ask, isn't function so central to what we are that making restrictions on function can only be seen as judgment on one's being? For example, we don't feel we really know other people until we know what kind of work they do. This is why the unemployed or the handicapped often feel as if they are not regarded as fully human. To me, this seems like a negative and destructive trait of our society. We may be too much devoted to the importance of work. It remains true, however, that what we do identifies who we are. What we do gives meaning to our humanness.

I take my question to the Bible and notice that God also is known through His works. He is the God who acts. Imaging Him is impossible. To try to do so is a sin (Exod. 20:4). But He can be thought of as the One who brought His people out of Egypt and the One who continues to lead them, teach them, and protect them. When Israelite parents wanted to teach their children about God, they would recount what He had done. That's how He could be known. In the New Testament, there is no philosophical, abstract discussion of Jesus' humanity or of His deity. But there are four testimonies (the four Gospels) to what He did. He was known through His works. He revealed God's compassion for the world by what He did. He said, *"My Father is still working, and I also am working"* (John 5:17). In conclusion, He prayed, *"I glorified you on earth by finishing the work you gave me to do"* (John 17:4).

It is necessary, when placing people into their churchly functions, to take into consideration their mental capacity, physical energy, spiritual gifts, and levels of spiritual maturity. These factors have a significant bearing on the work that needs to be done. However, to make decisions on the basis of skin color, racial origin, family connection, physical appearance, or gender, is offensive and debasing. These human features are usually not germane to the service being considered. Such differences are not to be seen as qualifications for membership in the kingdom of God or for service in it. God created people with differences, and rather than being discriminated against, people should be appreciated and respected in their differences.

My satirical mood rises to the surface and I imagine this scene at a baseball team's spring training camp. The manager faces six new pitchers—three are left-handed and three are right-handed—and says, "Welcome to the club! I want you to know that we appreciate each one of you. We regard you as being of equal value to the team. However, our policy is that we field only right-handed players. We

So Now There Should Be Equality

have good reasons for this policy. The Bible often mentions God's right hand but never His left hand. Besides that, Jesus said, 'Let not your left hand know what your right hand is doing.' Obviously, people are expected to work with their right hands. So, the three of you who are left-handed need not waste any time on our training drills. We will keep you on our team, but you will be assigned to canteen duty, to launder team uniforms, and to manage our equipment. And I'm sure you will have a great year with us." Would this be equality? Wouldn't it, in baseball culture, be a drastic, unconscionable demotion?

I have argued that our God-given gifts are an integral aspect of who we are before God. To affirm that we are equal when it comes to being justified by faith but not equal when it comes to expressing that new way of life in service, is a contradiction of what has just been affirmed. If a woman is recognized as having a gift for effective ministry in the Church, if she has the spiritual graces required for such a service, if she takes pleasure in serving others, if she has a love for God which she wants to express in serving, then creating restrictions that limit her service opportunities seems like an insult to her. It also seems like an insult to God who made her to be the kind of person she is.

Chapter 11

Considering the Divergent Texts

THE THEME OF EQUALITY which I have traced through the Bible seems to be coherent. It also seems to agree well with the redemptive love of God, i.e., it harmonizes with the essential message of the Bible. However, there are some New Testament challenges to the doctrine of full equality. I will refer to three of these. In 1 Corinthians 11:3, the apostle Paul declares that *"the husband is the head of the wife."* In his discussion of worship, in 1 Corinthians 14:34-35, he says, *"women should be silent in the churches."* Then, in the discussion of church order in 1 Timothy 2:11-15, the writer teaches that women are to be quiet and submissive.

Considering the Divergent Texts

These three passages have usually been at the center of any discussion on the role of women in the Church. Do these passages nullify the position I have developed here? Are they exceptions to the principle of equality? In the earlier years of my ministry, while I was convinced of the full equality of women and men, I did not feel free to preach the implications of that equality because of the texts I have just cited. They seemed to deny what I had otherwise concluded to be true. I assume there are many men and women in the Church who still feel as I did then. It is their allegiance to the full authority of the Holy Scriptures which keeps them from embracing a position which may actually, humanly speaking, seem very right. I kept questioning to what extent these biblical reminders, apparently written to correct some localized problem, should be allowed to influence my overall view of the biblical message, and what kind of normative influence these texts should have over the Church today? My conviction now is that the doctrine of equality, as developed here, must be allowed to stand on its own feet. It is not good hermeneutics to start with these "exceptions" and then interpret the rest of the Scriptures to fit them. Further, it doesn't even seem correct to refer to these difficult texts as "exceptions." I do agree, however, that they have often been seen as diverging from the doctrine of equality.

We encounter such divergent ideas as well when we study other New Testament teachings. For example, in 1 Corinthians 7, the apostle presents serious cautions against the practice of marriage, but in 1 Timothy 4, the advice for younger widows is that they are to marry again. The apostle Paul argued against the practice of circumcision in his letter to the Galatians but decided that his new assistant, Timothy, should be circumcised before he could join their missionary team (Acts 16:3). The variant teachings on the role of women are no more difficult than the variations mentioned above. Such differences in the teaching of the New Testament should not be labeled as contradictions; they can usually be explained readily when cultural and textual factors, such as differences in time, environment, local practices, and the purpose and occasion for the writing, are considered.

My intention here is to explore the meaning of the challenging texts listed above. To begin with, it may be useful to point out that none of these passages says a woman must not preach, that a woman must not be a pastor, or that a woman must not be ordained. While each of the passages has been used to argue for such restrictions on women, such arguments are only interpretations or deductions from what the texts actually say.

A basic conviction to which I hold about interpretation is that scriptures such as these must be kept within their context. First of all, "context" refers to the social and cultural environment out of which these teachings come. Secondly, it refers to the literary setting in which we read the texts. Responsible scholarship and obedient Christian living requires that we try to determine their meaning within the flow of the teaching which the writer is developing.

The three passages I discuss here are, in a sense, similar. They deal with the same concern—order in the Church. In each case, the writer is concerned about

Considering the Divergent Texts

retaining the credibility of the Church, which, apparently, was being threatened by the radically new spirit of emancipation that was at work in the church that the apostles had founded. Women had little value and received little respect in Graeco-Roman culture. Judaism, too, encouraged the subordination of women and the domination of men. Christianity, however, was the women's liberation movement of the first century. As we know, new freedoms may get out of hand. Liberated people are not always able to handle their new opportunities with acceptable social discretion. That problem can be sensed in the New Testament. The Christian doctrine of equality was so radical, and was embraced with such enthusiasm by the women of that day, that dangerous tensions and troubles sprang up in the churches. The Christian gospel had undermined many social restrictions. It has also been suggested that Gnostic practices and other cultic traits were entering the Church because of the new openness, and that this is what the apostles were primarily concerned about. Scholars are still researching to determine how significant the Gnostic factor was. In the meantime, we will deal with what we see in the written scriptural context. I am suggesting that, when divisive and destructive tendencies in the Church were discerned and challenged by the apostolic writers, such admonitions do not alter the principle of full equality. Rather, they endorse the principle. Women, too, are responsible for their conduct. They, too, are responsible for working in harmony and in unity with the rest of the Church and for maintaining the good reputation of the Church in its pagan environment.

1 Corinthians 11:3

The husband is the head of the wife.

The order issue at stake here is the reputation of the Christian congregation within the larger Corinthian community. The entire passage (v. 1-16), which deals with the head covering of the women who pray or prophecy, has been difficult for modern readers to comprehend. While I am not confident that I grasp fully the intricacies of the apostle's logic, I present here my current view. It seems that Paul is constrained, because of the radical way in which some women asserted their freedom, to argue against the supremacy of women. However, it's difficult for him to do this because he desperately wants to avoid implying the subordination of women. Because of his basic conviction about the equality of men and women, he cannot simply endorse the authority of the old traditions which they have abandoned. And so his reasoning gets rather complex and convoluted. At the end of the passage, we are not quite sure what he has accomplished.

There are several cautions we must take as we seek to understand this passage. In the first place, we must not assume that this was written directly to the Christian women of today. Secondly, we must realize that Paul could hardly have had the modern corporation structure in mind when he spoke of the "head." To us, the head of an organization is the boss. The word probably did not mean that to Paul. Thirdly, Paul makes several allusions to their culture which we today do not fully understand. Consequently, our interpretation of this passage must always be somewhat tentative.

Considering the Divergent Texts

The simple assertion that the husband is the head of the wife contains two serious difficulties. The first problem is reflected in the translation I have quoted. Other translations speak of the "man" and the "woman." The choice of words makes an important difference; does the text speak about the gender relationship in the family or does it pronounce a general principle that applies to all male and female relationships? The problem is caused by the Greek vocabulary. The words which the apostle used can mean either "husband" and "wife" or "man" and "woman." It is the translator who decides how these words will read in English. My view is that those translations which treat this as a husband/wife issue are probably correct.

The second difficulty here is the meaning of "head." I have already stated what "head" probably does not mean. While the Greek word which Paul uses can sometimes mean something like "chief" or "ruler," it does not mean that in most of its New Testament usages. A good example of the figurative way in which "head" is used is Ephesians 4:15-16, where the writer reminds his readers:

> *But speaking the truth in love, we must grow up in every way into him who is the head, into Christ, from whom the whole body, joined and knit together....*

Christ is similarly entitled as "head" in verses such as Ephesians 1:22-23 and Colossians 1:16-18. These verses seem to say that Christ holds all things together; He is the creative, integrative life force by which all things exist. While Christ is, of course, the Lord of the Church, these "head" passages do not seem to refer to His authoritative relationship to the Church; they speak, rather, of the new life factor of which He is the source and by which the Church exists.

The text we are studying here implies that there is a parallel between the husband being the head of the wife and God being the head of Christ. Rather than clarifying anything, this mystifies the issue. This takes us into the unfathomable mystery of the Trinity. Since the fourth century, the Church has generally agreed that Christ is not in any way less than fully God. The doctrine of subordination, which says that Christ is subordinate to the Father, has been seen as a false teaching. This judgment was established in response to the Arian threat. The aim of Arianism was to diminish the role of Christ, to make Him a lesser god, and to simplify the doctrine of God by establishing a divine hierarchy. The problem of how to express the relationship between God and Christ is still with us today. When I meet Jehovah's Witness teachers, who promote a modern-day version of subordinationism, they quote the words of Jesus, *"My Father is greater than I"* (John 14:28). I respond to that by explaining that those words were spoken by the incarnate Son when He was on earth in human form, and that the basic relationship is expressed by Jesus in John 10:30: *"I and my Father are one."* Who is right? If you agree with the Jehovah's Witness view that Christ is subordinate to God, you will find, in 1 Corinthians 11:3, support for the view that women are created below men. If you adhere to the traditional Christian doctrine of divine equality, you have at least one less problem with the view that women and men are equal.

In keeping with the divine relationship as it is developed in John's gospel (some helpful explanations about

Considering the Divergent Texts

the relationship between the Father and the Son are given by Jesus in John 14-16), I agree with those commentators who suggest that, when God is called the head of Christ, the writer is probably thinking of Christ's incarnation and of His sojourn here in human form. He has the origin of the human Christ in mind. That would then lead us to conclude that man is the head of the woman in the sense that he was made first, and she was made from his rib. The creation event was certainly in Paul's mind when he wrote this lesson; he mentions it again in verse 9. But he then seems to realize that his use of the creation theme may support the idea of male superiority, so he quickly qualifies his teaching in verse 11. An older male student said to me in class, "Wouldn't you agree that woman was made for man?" I disagreed, even though I am well aware that in 1 Corinthians 11:9, Paul says, *"Neither was man created for the sake of the woman, but woman for the sake of the man."* I disagreed because the apostle didn't mean what my student meant. It is exactly to avoid the kind of misconception expressed by the student that Paul qualified his previous statement by explaining:

> *Nevertheless in the Lord woman is not independent of man or man independent of woman. For just as woman came from man, so man comes through woman...* (v. 11-12).

There is an equality and equilibrium between the sexes. By the way, verse 9 could also be understood as meaning that the man was incapable of living by himself and needed a woman; in other words, the verse could be seen as reflecting the weakness of man. I believe, however, that what the apostle means is that in the Lord neither is independent of the other.

Whatever "head" means in verse 3, Paul does not use it here to argue for the supremacy of the male over the female. He does not say that the woman should address the Church only through her husband. He does not demand that a woman must not speak in the presence of men. His only concern is that her appearance, i.e., the way she covers her head, concurs with acceptable standards of decency and order. He does not want Christian women to be seen as cultural renegades. He does not want them to flaunt an unacceptable independence. And so he explains that she should have a proper covering when she prays or prophecies. This requirement is apparently based on Corinthian cultural values which, at this point, we do not fully understand. In any case, there is no hint that prophesying is out of order for the woman. If the apostle had believed that prophesying was inappropriate for a woman, he could have resolved the issue with one simple sentence and he would have saved himself a long and intricate expository lesson. As it is, Paul seems to say that the covered head gives her the authority to speak (v.10). For some reason, certain worship styles were a discredit to God. The apostle's concern is order; if women want to use their freedom to participate in public ministry, they should be thoughtful and do it responsibly.

Before I leave this topic, I should make a brief reference to the only other instance of the husband being called *"the head of the wife"* (Eph. 5:23). By the way, in neither passage is the husband commanded to be the head of the wife. The apostle does not treat it as an imperative or as a moral duty. It is simply a statement of fact. The Ephesians passage is easier to understand than the former. Here the husband is compared to Christ, who gave His life for the Church. Christ is seen here, not as the Lord of the Church, but as the Savior of the Church. There is, then, a very important lesson for the husband as well as for the wife. The passage begins with the prescript that believers are to be subject to one another (v. 21). Specifically, the wife is to respect and be submissive to her husband. The husband, on the other hand, is to love his wife as Christ loved the Church. Being the head here speaks more of care than of control, of responsibility than of privilege. Since Christ's redemptive work is the model, we could say that the husband's responsibility is to give his life, if need be, for the welfare of his wife.

1 Corinthians 14:34-35

> *Women should be silent in the churches. For they are not permitted to speak, but should be subordinate, as the law also says. If there is anything they desire to know, let them ask their husbands at home. For it is shameful for a woman to speak in church.*

The order issue, which concerns the apostle here, is that the congregation's worship time would be conducted in an edifying manner. The first Corinthian letter was written to bring a fragmenting Church together. This brief reminder in chapter 14 is part of that agenda. The reference to the prophesying of women in chapter 11 indicates that Paul accepted the public ministry of women provided they did it responsibly. He will not let the women, or the men, ruin the

Church with a self-seeking libertarian spirit. He fears that unrestrained and undisciplined freedom may result in confusion and discord. God's will, mentioned twice in chapter 14, is peace, harmony, and order (v. 33,40).

The advice Paul gives here about women also has a peculiar difficulty. The text refers to the law as the basis for the idea that women should be subordinate. However, there is no passage in the Old Testament that seems to match this reference. It is possible, then, that "law" refers to local customs of domestic propriety. Apart from this one enigmatic reference, however, it is easy to see what the apostle meant in this context. Earlier, the apostle has corrected other divisive practices: that believers would take fellow Christians to court (ch. 6); that women would prophecy with uncovered heads; that the communicants at the Lord's Supper divided and formed cliques (ch. 11). Now he mentions three new problems: 1) those who spoke in tongues used their gift even when no interpreters were present (v. 27-28); 2) prophets would compete with each other for time and prominence (v. 29-30); 3) women argued with their husbands in the worship service (v. 34-35).

For each problem, the apostle has clear counsel. The tongues speakers are to speak in turn, at the most three in one service, and they are to be silent if no interpreters are available. The prophets are to speak in order and defer to each other. All have the right to prophesy, but what is being said should be evaluated by the listeners. The women are to settle their differences with their husbands at home. The Greek word translated "speak" in verse 34 has, in the context (ch. 12,14), been used of tongues speaking; here it probably refers to domestic chatter that was adding to the chaos in their services. That this refers to domestic disputes in the Church and is not a blanket rejection of all female participation, seems likely because no provision is made for the singles in the Church. The controlling principle throughout the chapter is that all things should be done so that they build up (v. 26). This advice for women to be silent and in submission is fully consonant with the theme of 1 Corinthians. The Church was being ravaged by a divisive spirit of one-upmanship. The apostle writes to promote reconciliation. Worshippers should exhibit harmony, a harmony that would reflect the very nature of the God who is being worshiped.

1 Timothy 2:8-15

The order concern in this letter has to do with the danger of false teaching in the Church. Some scholars believe that the Pastoral Letters—1 Timothy, 2 Timothy, and Titus—diverge from the rest of the New Testament because they may have been written later, not by Paul but by a second-century compiler of Paul's ideas. I don't think such a drastic revision of traditional conviction is necessary. Rather, I suggest that these letters sound different because they were written late in Paul's life when some of the churches were in deep turmoil. His concern now is to protect the gospel which the apostles had preached against cultural influences that were already making deadly inroads into congregations. The section we are considering here also has some major difficulties that are often overlooked by those who use this text to support the traditional position on women. In the first place, it seems to say that women are saved by bearing children (v. 15). This comment is difficult to accept because it would keep single women and all infertile women from the benefit of salvation. Further, it contradicts the evangelical doctrine of salvation by grace for all those who believe. Consequently, most readers agree that this sentence cannot mean what it seems to be saying on the surface. Secondly, the text says, in verse 14, that Adam was not deceived but that the woman was and became a transgressor. This seems to place the blame for the introduction of sin on Eve. However, elsewhere Paul cites Adam as the originator of sin. What do we do with such anomalies?

Traditionally, interpreters have taken some lines in this passage literally and ignored the difficult sentences. I suggest that the whole section should be taken with equal seriousness. We should try to understand the situation that is being addressed and seek to discern what the original readers in Ephesus would have made of these admonitions. If we do this, I think we can agree that this passage does not contradict other New Testament teaching but that it adds a few more valuable details to the practice of Church harmony. The concern for order in the Church is here expressed as follows:

1) Men are to lift their hands in prayer without anger or argument (v.8).

2) Women are to dress modestly, focusing on good works rather than on outward appearance (v.9-10).

3) Women are to be silent in church. This, and the next two points, come out of the crucial section, verses 11 and 12.

Considering the Divergent Texts

Let a woman learn in silence with full submission. I permit no woman to teach or to have authority over a man; she is to keep silent.

The word "silent," which is here used twice, is the same as the word in 2:2 where it is usually seen as meaning peaceful. The term is probably not intended to mean that women are to be speechless in church. Rather, the idea is that, just as men must maintain proper decorum in church (v.8), women also must not be unruly or troublesome. This teaching reminds me of a woman in a congregation we were serving many years ago. She and her husband were new believers and had just moved to our town from a California city. One Sunday, they visited an adult class I was teaching. I had barely begun when she abruptly left the room. Something about her departure concerned my wife, and she followed her to the parking lot to ask if there was any problem. The young woman explained that she had noticed I expected the women in the class to participate in the discussion. However, the mentor who had guided her early Christian life had taught that women should not speak in church. She felt she had no right to say a word inside the church building. So she left before I would call upon her and embarrass her. We appreciated her sincerity and assured her we would respect her convictions. But we still think of that as a sad example of how believers can be misguided by a faulty interpretation of the biblical text.

4) Women must be in submission.

This is not a unique responsibility imposed only upon women. Submission is to be a common trait of believers, whether male or female (Eph. 5:21; Rom. 13:1,5; 1 Cor.

16:16; Titus 2:9; James 4:7; 1 Peter 5:5). Submission is not an unusual, exceptional attitude for women only. This statement simply includes women in the teaching given elsewhere to different classes of men; women too should live by this Christlike principle.

5) Women are not to teach or exercise authority over men (v.12).

This could hardly be a blanket prohibition of all teaching by women. Even though it seems to say that, very few churches have ever interpreted it that way. Teaching is usually regarded as a general responsibility which believers have toward each other (Col. 3:16). In fact, Timothy himself, the man who received this letter, learned his theology from two women, his mother and grandmother (2 Tim. 1:5, 3:15). This fact is mentioned without any negative connotations; Timothy is seen as being fortunate to have had such good teachers.

It is probably best to regard the two restrictions, "teach or have authority," as belonging together. Grammatically speaking, the second term would then define the kind of teaching forbidden for the women. The word translated "have authority" is used only this once in the New Testament. This makes it difficult to determine its exact meaning. However, elsewhere in Greek literature it has strong erotic and aggressive connotations. The restriction then fits with the advice on dressing modestly. The apostle's concern is that women not seduce men by improper dressing or mislead men with false teaching. That would explain the reference to Eve in verse 13. There once was a woman who was badly deceived and led her man into deep trouble. That the apostle would warn women against taking an authoritative,

Considering the Divergent Texts

dominant position of any kind over men makes good sense. Men shouldn't take such an attitude either. The picture of Church leadership in the Pastoral Epistles is that it must be gracious, non-argumentative, and servant-like (1 Tim. 6:3-11; 2 Tim. 2:15-16,23-26; Titus 3:1-2). Jesus taught that His disciples are to serve one another (Mark 10:43,45; Luke 22:24-27). The Pastoral Epistles take that servant concept and apply it to all members of the Church.

The Pastoral Letters give unusual attention to the threat of false teachings in the churches (see 1 Tim. 1:3-7; 4:1-5; 4:7; 6:3-5; 2 Tim. 2:14-18; 3:6-9; 4:3-4). The response to these heresies is to be rigorous adherence to the teachings of the apostles. "Sound doctrine" is the theme song of these letters (see 1 Tim. 1:10; 4:6; 4:16; 6:3; 2 Tim. 1:13; Titus 1:9; 2:1; 2:7). The fact that women are singled out specifically for admonition is understandable in view of the fact that some women had accepted false and destructive notions that were contrary to approved apostolic doctrine (see 1 Tim. 4:7; 5:11-15; 2 Tim. 3:6-7; Titus 2:3-5). Some women of that time seem to have been following the deceptive example set by Eve at the beginning. They should, rather, submit to sound doctrine and live a virtuous life. And that is exactly what these letters require of men as well.

That the main thrust of the Pastoral Letters is the preservation of true doctrine is readily seen by a quick reading of the letters. What exactly was the nature of heresy which concerned the writer is not that obvious. It is not given an official name. It is not described in any definitive way. Elsewhere in this book, I have referred to Gnosticism, that ambiguous amalgam of Platonic philosophy, Eastern mysticism, and Old Testament themes and characters which began to emerge in the first century. What is known about this movement would fit the references made in these letters.

In the first place, there was the Gnostic aversion to childbearing. Their dualistic views meant that flesh was seen as evil. Giving birth was considered to be a vile act because it brought more flesh to life. Any women who had given birth were seen as disgraced because of their contribution to the evil of the world. Such a view would explain the writer's emphatic argument for the value of having children.

The Pastoral Letters pay more specific attention to women than do the other letters. This, again, would be logical if the heresy that threatened was Gnosticism. Various historical references from the ancient Middle East show that Gnosticism was especially attractive to women. Earlier, I referred to the way some early Gnostic texts denigrate women. However, such a disparaging of females was not uniform. Even in the New Testament, we see evidences that feminist religions were prominent in Asia Minor. Ephesus was the center for the worship of Diana (Acts 18). The Lord's message to the church at Thyatira refers to a woman who called herself a prophet and was misleading the church with evil teachings (Rev. 2:20). It may have been such deviant feminist perversions which concerned the writer of the Pastoral Letters.

A common feature of Gnosticism was the re-imaging of the creation and temptation stories of Genesis 2 and 3. The Gnostics venerated knowledge. Eve was seen as having had the courage to bring knowledge to light. She had possessed the courage to embark on the path to enlightenment. She was, therefore, revered as the patron saint of

Considering the Divergent Texts

all those who were seeking for further knowledge. This would explain why 1 Timothy 2 makes such an emphatic declaration of Eve's sin and guilt.

What I am proposing with these explanatory paragraphs is that the best way to make sense of the theology of these letters is to assume the apostle is dealing here with a cultic perversion not found elsewhere. And what is known of Gnosticism gives us, at least, a hypothesis as to what was troubling the Church at that time. The same local conditions that caused the writer to make his uncharacteristic claims about the value of childbearing and the sinning of Eve, may have been behind the demand that women keep the peace and not try to dominate men

It seems highly ironic that the rigorous refutation of unsound teachings in the churches of Asia Minor seems to have contributed to the entrenchment of a male supremicism in the Church. By closing the door on one dangerous aberration, the writer opened the door to another. The spirit of equality which was evident early in the Church, soon gave way to the suppression of women.

Before I conclude this chapter, I must point out that even in these letters, women are expected to learn (1 Tim. 2:11). They are not written off as irrelevant; they are not to remain in ignorance. They too are to learn, grow, and develop. They too are to understand sound doctrine. There is a learning which is useless; the writer knows of women who are so captivated by sinful desires they will never be able to arrive at a knowledge of the truth (2 Tim. 3:6,7). However, there is nothing here of the rabbinic attitude which saw women as too unimportant and too unintelligent to learn theology.

Conclusion

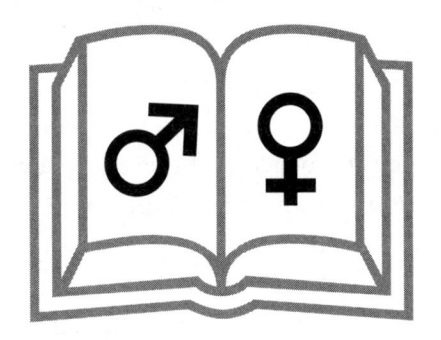

I MENTION AGAIN THE THREE-FOLD formula for the doctrine of equality which I have developed in this book. Men and women were created equal, according to Genesis 1 and 2; they were redeemed to be equal as declared by the summary statement of Galatians 3:28; they were confirmed in their equality when the Holy Spirit was granted to them at Pentecost, as described in Acts 2. With this biblical background in my mind, I ask three questions:

1) Since women and men are fully equal before God, shouldn't we let them be fully equal in the Church?

2) Since Christ died to save us from the effects of the

Conclusion

fall, shouldn't we appropriate His redemptive work and claim it, not only for our personal salvation but also for the healing of spoiled and damaged relationships, and stop trying to perpetuate a condition which Christ has terminated?

3) Since we agree that the Spirit came upon the whole Church and moves equally upon men and women, what right do we have to impose restrictions upon women which prevent them from using gifts they have received from the Spirit?

This paper does not claim that men and women are the same. Whatever psychological or physical differences they have is beside the point as far as the purpose of this book is concerned. I have argued that men and women should be allowed to work and serve in those areas in which they are gifted. This does not mean we must upset all conventions and enforce total reversibility of roles in the family, the Church, or society.

It must be granted that all human societies need structures in order to function in an orderly manner. All good parents know that children in the home need structure in order to create stability and a sense of security. The same is true of our Church communities. This is due to our humanness; in spite of our spiritual enlightenment in Christ, we are still relatively immature and corrupt. However, the structures we establish may, with time, become institutionalized to the point they are inflexible and bind people in their immaturity, keeping them from further development.

Now, what does all this say to two of the urgent questions facing evangelical churches today: Can a woman be allowed to preach? and can pastoral leadership be entrusted to a woman? In the Bible there is nowhere a direct affirmation nor a clear prohibition. The Bible does not ask the question the way we do today. If we look for simple texts to prove the case one way or another, the Bible seems to give mixed signals. This is not due to any uncertainty on God's part but to the fact that divine revelation comes to us through historical events and the cultures of a different time. So we have to seek God's will in the total canon of biblical literature, not only in a few selected texts. We must look in the Scriptures not only for simple rules but for principles we can use as we search for the right solutions to the issues of our times.

It may be helpful to remind ourselves that our concept of pastoral leadership is probably different from that which was held by the apostles and missionaries of the first century. When we think of pastoral leadership we tend to think of a single person presiding at the top of an administrative pyramid. The modern pastor is often seen as the CEO. Such a concept was unknown in the early Church. As the apostles saw it, the pastors worked alongside other gifted people. It seems, from the New Testament references, that churches had teams of pastors. In the apostles' minds then, a woman in pastoral leadership would never have been a lone leader; she would have been a member of a team. Further, Jesus had categorically rejected the innate human desire to be in a position of authority and dominance (Luke 22:24-27). Consequently, that a pastor would head up a hierarchy and preside over others, probably never entered the minds of the apostles when they identified the people who had pastoral gifts and appointed them to serve.

Conclusion

Let me briefly mention again the meaning of spiritual leadership which I developed in a previous chapter. Christian leadership is not about power over people. It's about ministry, serving others. It is the gift to influence others in a spiritual way. It's about following Jesus with the kind of joyful commitment that will encourage and motivate others to follow Him as well. It means reflecting the character of God and the love of Jesus Christ in such a way that others also desire to become Christlike in their attitudes and actions. Whenever a church assigns leadership on any other basis than these spiritual gifts and qualities, it is opening the door to the danger of abusive leadership.

The search for leadership with the necessary gifts means that a church cannot submit unthinkingly to the "myth of normality," whether that normality is that a pastor must be a young married man with a beautiful wife and two nice children, or that she must be a middle-aged single woman. First, the congregation must appraise the needs of the church. Then, it must look for the person who has the gifts to meet those needs.

The more traditional writers often refer to the problem of authority when they discuss the ministry of women. They argue that if a woman should be allowed to teach or preach she would have an authority which doesn't belong to her. I have read stern warnings about a woman not "usurping an improper authority." I wonder what is this "authority" which seems like such a dangerous threat to some Christian thinkers? When a minister works as a member of the congregation, functioning as one among many under the authority of the Word of God and of the Holy Spirit, and understands that being a minister is a servant role, there seems to be no room for an improper authority. When a church recognizes a person's preaching or teaching abilities and entrusts him or her with that ministry, that person does not become an authority figure. That person's authority is in the authoritative word which is being expounded. The Church is not like an army in which orders are arbitrarily imposed from the top. It is not a hierarchical structure as are some business corporations. It is a body, a fellowship of believers. Some of these believers have gifts for one ministry, some for another; as they serve under the Lordship of Jesus Christ, the Holy Spirit will lead the Church through them. True ministers of Christ don't desire authority to lord it over others, and they don't seek for it in their ministry. They are servants. The Church should not think of ministers as having an authoritarian role. So we should respond to the concern mentioned above, "Yes, ministers must be careful that they do not assume an improper authority. But the danger you express is not unique to females. It must be heeded by all those who serve, in any role or function."

One matter of particular concern, the ordination of women, is not addressed by the Scriptures at all. The New Testament does not know of ordination as we think if it. Ordination is an ecclesiastical concept, developed over the centuries to regulate ministry in the Church. If we want to discuss ordination in the light of biblical principles, we should always first ask, "What is the meaning of ordination in our church? For what purpose do we ordain people?" The issue is not simply whether women can be ordained, but what women can be allowed to do in church. The question about ordination is really a secondary issue.

Conclusion

I am not surprised that many churches in our day look for a male pastor when they search for leadership. Even churches that agree totally with the principle of equality may thoughtfully decide that their church could better do God's will with a male pastor than with a female leader. Such a decision might be due to the traditions out of which they have come; they may decide to be careful about making a wrenching departure from the customs of the past. It might be made because of local community values which require that institutions be led by males. It might seem necessary due to local prejudices which would keep a church from attracting new people if it were pastored by a woman. It might simply be due to the type of demands which that church places upon its pastor. The congregational decision to limit a pastoral choice to males would, in such cases, not necessarily contradict biblical precedents. There are many examples in the New Testament of an important principle that is clearly affirmed, but then suspended because of local conditions. For example, the apostle Paul believes marriage is good but advises against it in 1 Corinthians 7. He argues that an idol is nothing (1 Cor. 8), but then warns that idolatry should be avoided (1 Cor. 10). The Jerusalem Council (Acts 15) decided that Jewish regulations should not be imposed upon Gentile believers, but then listed four exceptions to the rule. It seems to be quite common to have a basic rule but then recognize that temporal, regional, or cultural factors require exceptions be made. However, when we make such exceptions, we should still affirm the basic biblical principles that apply. We should not change the principles or create new principles, because of local or personal concerns.

By granting the concession above, I do not intend to alter or weaken in any way the basic argument of this book. However, there are two New Testament principles which lead me to grant that such a compromise between policy and practice may sometimes be necessary. Both of these have to do with the problem of being the Church in the world. The first principle is that freedom must be used with discretion. The apostle explained, in 1 Corinthians 6, that, while all things may be lawful for him, he will not be dominated by anything. In other words, he will not become a slave of freedom. In Galatians 5, he argues for the absolute imperative of freedom from Jewish law. *"Stand firm, therefore, and do not submit again to the yoke of slavery"* (v.1). But then he admonishes them to manage their freedom carefully and use it to serve one another in love. So, while there is no theological reason why women should be excluded from church ministries, a sensitive church body might agree that God's will would be served better by moving ahead with discretion. And women might, in their freedom, make the thoughtful and responsible decision to defer from demands which might damage the Church.

A second principle is that a church must always consider itself accountable to its own people. Its own people may have problems with unexamined prejudices, whether based on denominational, racial, ethnic, or gender distinctions. While such prejudices may be evil and in need of outright rejection, they must be dealt with in a way that will lead to the betterment of the church rather than its destruction.

To those who feel that their convictions about equality are being discriminated against in their own congregations, I counsel patience. Many of those who are speaking up

Conclusion

against female leadership may sincerely be seeking to understand and obey God's will. It may be easier to be patient if we can recall the power that various customs and traditions used to have over us. Most of us can remember convictions we once had which, with the passing of time, with the influence of new experiences, with the insight of more mature reflection, have now been respectfully laid aside. Further, we must realize that people often have strong feelings about important matters. These feelings may not have any biblical basis, but they may, nevertheless, be quite real and very troubling. I recall the senior person who once admonished me for asking women to read the Scriptures in church. He agreed he could not find any biblical reason for his concern. "But," he said, "it just doesn't feel right." I admired his honesty, and I am glad that he is still participates actively in a church in which women can read the Bible in public as freely as men do.

Too often, people assume that their feelings are God-given and they tend to distort and misuse biblical teachings to defend those feelings. What we have inherited usually feels right to us. So I am not at all surprised that people have strong feelings about women in leadership. I recall various strong feelings I have had which, at one time, seemed unquestionably right. Feelings are very personal. They are integral to who we are. We cannot expect people simply to disregard their feelings. Fortunately, however, feelings about right and wrong may change. But that usually takes time.

For those who feel threatened by the emergence of women leaders in their churches, I counsel tolerance. Please recognize the lesser significance of this issue in contrast to the many great doctrines of the faith on which we can agree. Can't we be as gracious about this as Paul said we should be about the questions concerning the keeping of holy days or the eating of meat? After explaining that it is normal to have differing convictions about such issues he asks,

Why do you pass judgment on your brother or sister? Or you, why do you despise your brother or sister? For we will all stand before the judgment seat of God (Rom. 14:10).

Having different views about the leadership of women is also not an issue over which we should despise, judge, or condemn one another. And it is certainly not an issue over which the Church should divide. It is a sign of spiritual immaturity when one side or the other threatens to split over such disagreements. We are one because we have one hope, one Lord, one faith, one baptism, and one Father who is above all of us (Eph. 4:4-6). To threaten, or to fear, church divisions over the issue of women in ministry betrays a serious ignorance about what is important to God and a misunderstanding of the foundation of our unity.

With this, I hark back once more to one of my opening concerns. The Church is to be directed by the Holy Spirit. In all of our deliberations let us never forget this. Let us remember that we are human and that humans make mistakes. So let us never make decisions or formulate policies that would keep the Spirit from reminding us of error if that should be necessary. Let us never act as if our present convictions are infallibly correct. Let

Conclusion

us never close our eyes to new visions for service and witness that the Lord may have for us. May Christ be Lord in His own body! May the Holy Spirit fill us with the grace of Christ! And may we yield to His leading!

For Further Reading

This list of books is a representative selection of resources, produced by scholars and Church leaders from a wide ecclesiastical perspective, which will be useful for further reading and research on the theme of this book. It also represents some of the key sources, beside the Holy Scriptures, that have informed me as I reflected on the issue of equality.

Background Resources

Arlandson, James Malcolm. *Women, Class, and Society in Early Christianity*. Peabody, Mass.: Hendricksen Publishers, 1997.

For Further Reading

Bullough, Vern; Shelton, Brenda; and Slavin, Sarah. *The Subordinated Sex*. Athens, Georgia: The University of Georgia Press, 1988.

Heine, Susanne. *Women and Early Christianity*. Minneapolis: Augsburg Publishing House,1988.

Kroeger, Richard Clark, and Kroeger, Catherine Clark. *I Suffer Not a Woman*. Grand Rapids: Baker Book House, 1992.

Pagels, Elaine. *The Gnostic Gospels*. New York: Vintage Books, 1981.

Biblical Interpretation

Fee, Gordon D. *Gospel and Spirit: Issues In New Testament Hermeneutics*. Peabody, Mass.: Hendricksen Publishers, 1991.

Fee, Gordon D. and Stuart, Douglas. *How to Read the Bible for All It's Worth*. Grand Rapids: Zondervan Publishing House, 1993.

Mickelsen, A. Berkley and Mickelsen, Alvera M. *Better Bible Study*. Glendale, California: Regal Books,1977.

Sire, James W. *Scripture Twisting*. Downers Grove, Illinois: InterVarsity Press, 1980

Swartley, Willard M. *Slavery, Sabbath, War and Women: Case Histories in Biblical Interpretation*. Scottdale, Pennsylvania. Herald Press, 1992.

Sexual Equality

Bilezikian, Gilbert. *Beyond Sex Roles*. Grand Rapids: Baker Book House, 1986.

Cowles, C. S. *A Woman's Place?* Kansas City: Beacon Hill Press, 1993.

France, R. T. *Women in the Church's Ministry.* Grand Rapids: William B. Eerdmans Publishing Company, 1995.

Grenz, Stanley. *Women in the Church.* Downers Grove, Ill.: InterVarsity Press, 1995.

Haubert, Katherine. *Women As Leaders: Accepting the Challenge of Scriptures.* Monrovia, Cal.: MARC, 1993.

Martin, Faith. *Call Me Blessed.* Grand Rapids: William B. Eerdmans Publishing Co.: 1988.

Maxwell, L. E. *Women in Ministry.* Wheaton: Victor Books, 1987.

Smith, Marilyn B. *Gender or Giftedness.* World Evangelical Fellowship on Women's Concerns, 2000.

Van Leeuwen, Mary Stewart. *After Eden: Facing the Challenge of Gender Reconciliation.* Grand Rapids: William B. Eerdmans Publishing Company, 1993.

Volf, Miroslav. *Exclusion and Embrace.* Nashville: Abingdon Press, 1996.

Witherington III, Ben. *Women and the Genesis of Christianity.* Cambridge: Cambridge University Press, 1990.